God in the Present Tense

God in the Present Tense

The Person and Work of the Holy Spirit

by

D. Shelby Corlett

Beacon Hill Press of Kansas City
Kansas City, Missouri

Copyright, 1974
Beacon Hill Press of Kansas City

Printed in the
United States of America

Permission to quote from copyrighted versions of the Bible is acknowledged as follows:
Revised Standard Version of the Bible (RSV), copyrighted 1946 and 1952.
The Amplified New Testament, copyright 1958 by the Lockman Foundation, La Habra, Calif.
New American Standard Bible (NASB), copyright © The Lockman Foundation, 1960, 1962, 1963, 1968, 1971.
The New English Bible (NEB), © the Delegates of the Oxford University Press and the Syndics of the Cambridge University Press, 1961, 1970.
The New Testament in Modern English (Phillips), copyright © by J. B. Phillips, 1958. Used by permission of the Macmillan Co.
The Bible: An American Translation (Goodspeed), by J. M. Powis Smith and Edgar J. Goodspeed. Copyright 1923, 1927, 1948 by the University of Chicago Press.
The Bible: A New Translation (Moffatt) by James Moffatt. Copyright 1954 by James Moffatt. Used by permission of Harper and Row, Publishers, Inc.
Today's English Version of the New Testament (TEV). Copyright © American Bible Society, 1966.
The New Testament: A New Translation, Vol. 1, by William Barclay. Copyright 1968 by William Collins Sons and Co., Ltd., London.

Contents

Preface	7
1. God in the Present Tense	9

Who Is the Holy Spirit? ○ How Does God Work with Man? ○ Prevenient Grace ○ Saving Grace ○ Entire Sanctification ○ Filled with the Holy Spirit ○ Some Spiritual Disciplines

2. Sanctified by the Holy Spirit	36

The Baptism with the Holy Spirit ○ The Person Is All-important ○ God Is at Work in Us ○ One Life: Two Experiences

3. A New Life-style	54

A Challenge to Reach the Best ○ The Christian Fellowship ○ Children of Hope ○ We Live in the World

4. Life in Relation	74

The Meaning of Love ○ The Obedience of Love ○ Responsible Christians ○ Humility and Penitence

5. Called unto Holiness	87

God Calls Us to Holiness ○ The Will of God ○ What the Call to Holiness Means ○ He Gives to Us His Holy Spirit

6. We Belong to God	109

Does God Have a Word for Us? ○ The Act of Consecration ○ Sanctified by Faith ○ God's Provision for Us

7. The Day of Pentecost   121
    The Day of Fulfillment o Who Were Filled with the
    Spirit? o Their Need to Be Spirit-filled o Their
    Preparation for Pentecost o The Promise Fulfilled o
    A Corporate Experience o The Promise Extended
    o Peter's Experience o Other Pentecostal Experiences

8. The Spirit-filled Life   142
    What Has the Spirit Brought to Us? o It Is a Spirit-
    filled Life o Life in Relationship with God's People o
    The Gifts of the Spirit o The Resources of the Spirit

Reference Notes   157

Preface

From my early childhood I have been under the wholesome influence and teaching of such people as my parents, pastors, evangelists, college professors, and have had the association of the finest teachers and preachers of the holiness movement in America, including the leaders of the Church of the Nazarene. They have given me what I believe to be a reasonable interpretation of the Bible and of the teachings of the church, and have also been examples in living of the doctrine of entire sanctification through the baptism with the Holy Spirit.

I am grateful for the opportunity I had of preparing the gist of the material in this book for a series of studies with the Adult Department of the Sunday school of the Riverside, Calif., Arlington Avenue Church of the Nazarene in the spring of 1972. The Book Committee of our church, after reviewing the notes used in those studies, requested me to write this fuller treatment for publication, and I appreciate the privilege thus afforded, for it has been one of the most enjoyable endeavors I have ever undertaken. Above all, I am deeply grateful to God for His love and grace, His patience and loving-kindness, and His gracious presence and help throughout my life; and to the Church of the Nazarene, which has given me opportunities for service which I felt were always beyond my capabilities, but which I endeavored to fill by the help of God; and for the fellowship, patience, and understanding I have received from the brethren over the years.

The message of this book may be considered the summary of my lifetime (I am now in my eightieth year) of study and writing and preaching of this doctrine. I pray earnestly that God will make the message effective in giving people a clearer understanding of this doctrine, that many will be led by the Spirit into the personal experience of the baptism with the Holy Spirit, and that many who are now living the life of holiness may be inspired to a closer walk with Christ and to a more fruitful life of service for Him as they live in our present evil world.

—D. Shelby Corlett
Duarte, Calif.

Chapter

ONE

God in the Present Tense

When are we in the presence of God? God is omnipresent; He fills the universe with His presence. But in a personal way He is always present with all persons everywhere and at all times. The Psalmist was inspired by this thought when he wrote:

> *Whither shall I go from thy spirit? or whither shall I flee from thy presence? If I ascend up into heaven, thou art there: if I make my bed in hell, behold, thou art there. If I take the wings of the morning, and dwell in the uttermost parts of the sea, even there shall thy hand lead me, and thy right hand shall hold me. If I say, Surely the darkness shall cover me; even the night shall be light about me. Yea, the darkness hideth not from thee; but the night shineth as the day: the darkness and the light are both alike to thee* (Ps. 139: 7-12).

When God is actively at work in the world and with men, this activity is the activity of the Spirit of God, the Holy Spirit. From the dawn of creation when "the Spirit of

God moved upon the face of the waters" (Gen. 1:2) until "The Spirit and the bride say, Come" (Rev. 22:17), the Spirit of God has been and is and will be working in the world and with man.

Who Is the Holy Spirit?

To think of the Holy Spirit brings to our minds the Divine Trinity: Father, Son, and Holy Spirit. Our creedal statement is: "We believe in one eternally existent, infinite God, Sovereign of the universe . . . that He, as God, is Triune in essential being, revealed as Father, Son, and Holy Spirit" (*Manual,* 1972, p. 27).

The Divine Trinity is a trinity of revelation, for the Bible reveals God as a trinity in His nature and in His actions with men in history. And it is a trinity of experience, for God makes himself known and works with man in a triune manner. At best the Divine Trinity is a mystery beyond the ability of the mind of man to fathom. But we all know that if we could understand God He would not be the God we need.

The well-known Apostles' Creed says, "I believe in God the Father Almighty, Maker of heaven and earth," because God has revealed himself as the Creator. We also say, "I believe in God the Redeemer," because He has revealed himself in His Son, Jesus Christ, who has redeemed us with His precious blood. And we say, "I believe that God is very active in our world and in my life now as the Holy Spirit." Although we may be unable to fathom the mystery of this triune God, we may enjoy the blessings He brings to us in these revelations He gives of His nature and person.

There are no analogies adequate to explain the Divine Trinity. However there are some factors of life which give us a hint of what might be meant by His being triune in essential being. Some time ago a friend and I visited in a home of people whom I had not met before. Three ladies were present at that time, an older woman, one middle-aged, and a younger one. In their conversation the older woman spoke of her son and of some things he did. At times the middle-aged woman spoke of her husband and his activities. And occasionally the younger woman spoke of her father and his life. At first I thought there were three different men. But as I listened I realized they were talking about the same man. He was the son of the older woman, the husband of the middle-aged woman, and the father of the younger woman. That did not make the man three different persons; it revealed him in three different relationships—son, husband, and father. But he was one man. I think we must have something of this nature in our thinking when we consider the Divine Trinity. There are not three Gods, but as our creed says, there is "One God . . . revealed as Father, Son, and Holy Spirit."

The classical theological statements of the Divine Trinity have been and are of great value and we need them, but for our purpose let us consider some practical statements by recent writers. Dr. Georgia Harkness gives this statement of the Trinity:

> The Father is the loving and almighty Maker of heaven and earth, infinite in wisdom, power, goodness and love. The Son is the same God incarnate in Jesus Christ as the Revealer of God and the Savior of men. The Holy Spirit is the same God, infinite and eternal, acting in our lives, present with us, here and now.

Dr. Elton Trueblood in one of his books says of the Trinity: "The Father is God in creation; the Son is God in history; the Holy Spirit is God in the present tense."

That is it! *God in the present tense.* The Holy Spirit

is God acting in our lives, present with us, here and now. He is actively at work in our world today.

What is the Holy Spirit's work with man in our world today? We at least get a hint of His work today from the statement of our creed as it is found in the ritual for the reception of members:

> We believe that man is born in sin; that he needs the work of forgiveness through Christ and the new birth by the Holy Spirit; that subsequent to this there is the deeper work of heart cleansing or entire sanctification through the infilling of the Holy Spirit (*Manual*, 1972, p. 310).

This is the same as saying that, after the work of the Holy Spirit in the new birth, man needs the further work of the Spirit in heart cleansing, or entire sanctification. The emphasis here is that the Holy Spirit, God in the present tense, is a Person who is now actively working with man, who is born in sin.

How Does God Work with Man?

God begins with man as he is, with man in a state which is very opposite to that of having a clean heart, and continues to work with him until the work of heart cleansing is completed.

What is meant by saying, "Man is born in sin"? Man is born into the world humanly alive but spiritually dead. That is, he has physical life, mental capacities, and other capabilities for his normal advancement and development as an individual in this world, but he is not alive to God spiritually.

There is something fundamentally wrong in the very center of human life, and this something wrong is not the result of that man's actions. It is something deep in the very nature of mankind, something which he shares with all other persons in the world, for all men are born in sin. It is the universal tendency of man to turn to his own ways in a self-centered life rather than to follow the ways of God; so then he becomes a sinner by his own acts.

Paul stated this wrongness or sin in man clearly in Rom. 5:12: "It was through one man that sin gained an entry into the world, and through sin came death, and so death passed to all men, because all had sinned" (Barclay).

This means that whatever is a man's background, however well-bred or ill-bred he is, whatever his color or race, man is born in sin and hence is in a state of spiritual death. This is our actual human situation as we are born into this world.

What do we mean by death—this death that spread to all men? Death means the absence of life; in physical death, physical life comes to an end. Man is spiritually dead because he is born with the absence of spiritual life. But death is more. If death were only the absence of life, we could keep the bodies of our dead loved ones around indefinitely. Death is not only the absence of life, but means the presence of an active process of decay or dissolution. Within a very short time a dead body deteriorates into the condition which described Lazarus (John 11:39). Just so, death in the spiritual sense is not only the absence of spiritual life; it includes a moral state of decay which inevitably leads man to do wrong or to sin. He becomes a slave to sin. Man is born into this world deprived of spiritual life, and he becomes depraved through the active process of spiritual and moral decay.

We do well always to keep in mind that man was made in the image of God, and although that image is marred because man has sinned, the image of God is not destroyed. There is something fundamental in man which morally distinguishes him from the animal creation—something related to God to which He can appeal as He works with man, who is born in sin. And indeed God does so work with man.

PREVENIENT GRACE

God has intervened in His grace through the gift of His Son, Jesus Christ, to help man in his sinful state. Let us look at some words from the Apostle Paul in Rom. 5:15:

> *For if one man's offense made the mass of mankind die, God's mercy and his gift given through the favor of the one man Jesus Christ have more powerfully affected mankind* (Goodspeed). Or,

> *It was by the generosity of God, the free giving of the grace of one man Jesus Christ, that the love of God overflowed for the benefit of all mankind* (Phillips).

This action of God is called Prevenient Grace; something antecedent to human action; grace before human action; God intervening before man himself was able to act. As Paul says elsewhere in that chapter, "For when we were yet without strength, in due time Christ died for the ungodly. . . . God commendeth his love toward us, in that, while we were yet sinners, Christ died for us" (Rom. 5:6, 8). He is saying that God has intervened for man, who is born in sin, and that what He has done is as extensive as is the human need. All men have sinned, but the work of Jesus Christ has "powerfully affected mankind," and God working through our gracious Saviour has brought benefits overflowing to all men. No man, whatever his moral or spiritual state, is excluded from these benefits of God's grace.

What would happen if God were not intervening in our world today? We have much wickedness in the world now, but how much more we would have if God were not intervening! Let us recognize that without God's intervention man in his unrestrained sin, in his depravity, would have brought utter destruction upon our race. Man would have sunk in his depravity to depths beyond the possibility of redemption. Total death—physically, morally, and spiritually—would exist. Mankind would become as wicked as it is capable of becoming. But God has intervened and man is restrained; he is surrounded by the prevenient grace of God, and as Dr. H. Orton Wiley has said, "This gift of grace in Jesus Christ to all men is the first benefit of the universal atonement made by Jesus Christ."

Prevenient grace is the presence, guidance, and influence of God's Spirit—God in the present tense. Even in early human history when man had become so evil God wanted to destroy him, it was said, "My spirit shall not always strive with man" (Gen. 6:3). This means that from the very beginning of sin in the human race, the Spirit of God has been influencing and working with man. God did not destroy man; rather He strove with man in his sin. He worked with him to influence him toward righteousness and God.

Another scripture which speaks of prevenient grace is that relating to the coming of Jesus into the world when the Word was made flesh to dwell among us. It says that Jesus "was the true Light, which lighteth every man that cometh into the world" (John 1:9). Note the words "every man." This tells us that, while every man coming into the world is born in sin and is deprived of spiritual life, he is not deprived of the presence of the grace of God. Every man is lighted by the true Light, Jesus, who came into the world. The presence of God surrounds man's life; God works with him; the Spirit of God moves upon him. This is prevenient grace, grace that comes before human action.

Paul speaks about God working with the Gentiles as follows:

> *When the gentiles, who have no knowledge of the Law [i.e., God's revealed law given to the Jews], act according with it by the light of nature, they show that they have a law in themselves, for they demonstrate the effect of a law operating in their hearts. Their own consciences endorse the existence of such a law, for there is something which condemns or excuses their actions* (Rom. 2:14-15, Phillips).

This means that every man has within him something that tells him what is right and what is wrong. Perhaps it is related to the fact that man was made in the image of God. Although the image is marred by sin, the law of God is still written in the hearts of mankind. This is the basis for the desire in people to be good, to do good works, and to help other people, even when they do not have spiritual life. It indicates that the grace of God is working with them.

This working of God with man born in sin is the prevenient grace of God. Because of this grace, babies and mentally irresponsible persons are under the covenant of grace and are saved. On the other hand, the response a normal person gives to the influence of God's Spirit working upon him (to this prevenient grace) determines the kind of moral life that person lives. If he fails to respond favorably, he becomes more and more sinful and depraved; if he gives a more favorable response, his life and character are governed by high moral ideals and good works toward his fellowman. It is the nature of this response which makes our associates and neighbors who are without God's saving grace live as good or as evil people.

But as beneficial as is this prevenient grace, it is not

saving grace. Man is saved only through the grace of God as he "turn[s] from sin to righteousness, [and] believe[s] on Jesus Christ for pardon and cleansing from sin" (*Manual,* 1972, p. 30). Even under the powerful influence of the intervening grace of God, man is still dead spiritually.

Saving Grace

Because man is born in sin, he becomes a sinner who "needs the work of the Holy Spirit in regeneration," for "all have sinned, and come short of the glory of God" (Rom. 3:23). A sinner is a person who keeps God out of his life, one who refuses to yield to the will of God, however "good" he may be otherwise. There are "up-and-out" sinners as well as down-and-out ones—*all* have sinned. But the good news is that *all* are offered the work of the Holy Spirit in regeneration.

How man becomes a sinner is described by Paul in his account of his own experience with sin. What he depicts is the experience of every man:

> *I would not have known what sin is unless through the action of the law [i.e., until I became a responsible person facing the law]. What I mean is, I would not have known what it is to covet unless the law said: "You must not covet." It was through the commandment that sin found a bridgehead in me, and thus awakened in me all kinds of wrong desires. . . . I once enjoyed life in a state in which I knew nothing about the law [i.e., in a state of innocence]. Then the commandment came into my life [i.e., I was awakened to responsible living] and sin sprang to life, and life became death for me [i.e., I lost my state of innocence]. . . . It was through the commandment [i.e., through my facing responsibility and failing]*

that sin gained a bridgehead in me, and seduced me, and through it for me turned life into death. . . . We know the law is spiritual [i.e., its demands are right] but I am made of flesh and blood. I have been sold into sin's slavery. My own actions are a mystery to me. What I do is not what I want to do but what I hate to do. . . . The fact is that it is not I who do it, it is sin who has made its home in me (Rom. 7:7-17, Barclay).

Note Paul's statement about coveting (v. 7). Paul's natural instinct for possessing things met head on with the commandment, so he said:

I should never have felt guilty of the sin of coveting if I had not heard the Law saying, "Thou shalt not covet." But the sin in me, finding in the commandment an opportunity to express itself [through having a natural instinct perverted to its own end], stimulated all my covetous desires" (vv. 7-8, Phillips).

This is sin's way of working, to pervert man's natural instincts toward the ends of sin. This was Satan's approach to Eve in Eden (Gen. 3:5-6). He used her natural instinct for knowledge—"Your eyes shall be opened, and ye shall be as gods, knowing good and evil. . . . a tree to be desired to make one wise." He also appealed to her instinct for physical preservation—"The tree was good for food"—and to her aesthetic nature—it was "pleasant to the eyes" or "tempting to contemplate" (NEB). He directed these naturally good impulses toward disobedience to God's law, toward sin, and she "did eat." She became a sinner, and her husband followed her in this disobedience.

The sinful condition of man is further described by Paul as being "dead in trespasses and sins." Or, as Phillips translates it, "You . . . were spiritually dead all the time that you drifted along on the stream of this world's ideas of living, and obeyed its unseen ruler (who is still operating in those who do not respond to the truth of God)" (Eph. 2:1-2).

These scriptures describe how people become sinners and the condition in which they live.

But again God has intervened. As once He intervened by surrounding man with His prevenient grace, He now intervenes by offering to man born in sin His saving grace.

Let us look at some of the scriptures which tell of this marvelous saving grace of God:

"God commendeth his love toward us, in that, while we were yet sinners, Christ died for us" (Rom. 5:8). "Who [Christ] in his own self bare our sins in his own body on the tree, that we, being dead to sins, should live unto righteousness" (1 Pet. 2:24). "For Christ also hath once suffered for sins, the just for the unjust, that he might bring us to God" (1 Pet. 3:18). "In whom we have redemption through his blood, even the forgiveness of sins" (Col. 1:14).

Through our Lord and Saviour Jesus Christ, God has intervened for sinners in that He has made provision for the salvation of all men, for the forgiveness of sins and the work of the Holy Spirit in regeneration. Hence man, who is born in sin and is dead in trespasses and sins, through these provisions of saving grace made by Jesus Christ may be made alive spiritually through faith in Him.

Let us consider *the work of God in regeneration.* There is an example given of this work of the Spirit in the conversation of Jesus with Nicodemus (John 3:1-16). Nicodemus was a religious leader of the Jews; he had profited much from his response to prevenient grace and its influences as well as from his religious instructions. He came to talk with Jesus about religious matters. Jesus surprised him by saying, "Except a man be born again . . . be born of the

Spirit, he cannot enter into the kingdom of heaven" (vv. 3, 5). To be born of the Spirit is the same as "the work of the Holy Spirit in regeneration." How could a religious leader, spiritually dead, become alive spiritually? By being "born again" through the Spirit's work of regeneration.

Paul in writing to Titus said:

Not by works of righteousness which we have done, but according to his mercy he saved us, by the washing of regeneration, and renewing of the Holy Ghost; which he shed on us abundantly through Jesus Christ our Saviour; that being justified by his grace, we should be made heirs according to the hope of eternal life (3:5-7).

What happens when the Holy Spirit—God in the present tense—regenerates a person who was born in sin? Here are some scriptural thoughts which tell what happens:

Regeneration, or being born again, makes a person a child of God by grace and frees him from the bondage of sin (Rom. 6:14). The love of God is shed abroad in his heart by the Holy Spirit, who is given unto him as he is justified by faith (Rom. 5:1, 5). He is led by the Spirit and has the Spirit of adoption, whereby he cries, "Abba, Father," and he is assured of his sonship by the witness of the Spirit to his spirit that he is a child of God (Rom. 8:15-16). He is given the Spirit of Christ, for he knows that if anyone has not the Spirit of Christ he is none of His (Rom. 8:9). He is made to realize that his body is the temple of the Holy Spirit, who is in him (1 Cor. 6:19). Because he is a son, God has sent the Spirit of His Son into his heart, crying, "Abba, Father" (Gal. 4:6).

One of the most wonderful factors of the regenerated life is that the Holy Spirit is dwelling in one's heart, making the life totally different to what it was before. "The Holy Spirit . . . is given" unto him (Rom. 5:5).

Dr. J. B. Chapman said: "As the heart is renewed by the active agency of the Holy Spirit, the Holy Spirit himself dwells within the believer's heart as 'the Spirit of adoption'; and by his presence alone is the Christian life continued in reality" (*The Holy Spirit*, p. 11).

John Wesley said:

> In speaking of a "second change", of "being saved from all sin and perfected in love," if they want to call this receiving the Holy Spirit, they may; only the phrase in that sense, is not scriptural, and not quite proper; for they all received the Holy Spirit when they were justified. God then sent forth the Spirit of his Son into their hearts, crying, "Abba, Father." (Quoted by Daniel Steele in *A Defense of Christian Perfection*, p. 108.)

How is a sinner "born again"? By the aid of the Holy Spirit he repents of his sins or turns utterly from sin to God and righteousness; he realizes that God through Christ, the Saviour, has provided spiritual life for him; he believes on the Lord Jesus Christ, that He is trustworthy, that "he is faithful and just to forgive" him his sins (1 John 1:9); and through his believing or faith in Christ he accepts Him as his personal Saviour. He is "born again" of the Holy Spirit, who is given to him. This change is so marvelous and radical that Paul describes it in these words: "If any man be in Christ, he is a new creature: old things are passed away; behold, all things are become new" (2 Cor. 5:17). And again, God "hath delivered us from the power of darkness, and hath translated us into the kingdom of his dear Son" (Col. 1:13).

This work of the Holy Spirit in regeneration is a marvelous experience for the man who is born in sin. Anything that can bring spiritual life to a person who is dead in trespasses and sins; anything that can break the power of sin upon his life and enable him to live righteously in this world; anything that can deliver him from the power of darkness and transfer him to the kingdom of Christ, belongs to what is called "so great salvation" (Heb. 2:3). There is never a need to minimize this work of the Holy Spirit in regeneration in order to make room for His further work in entire sanctification. It is a life in which there is growth and development in Christ, although there is also an awareness of the need of a deeper experience of grace.

Entire Sanctification

Let us now look at the other thought in the *Manual* statement under consideration, namely, "That subsequent to this [that is, the new birth by the Holy Spirit] there is the deeper work of heart cleansing or entire sanctification through the infilling of the Holy Spirit" (p. 310). Also note our creedal statement on entire sanctification that "it is wrought by the baptism with the Holy Spirit" (*Manual*, 1972, p. 31). In other words, we believe that the baptism with the Holy Spirit and entire sanctification are one and the same experience.

We have noted that the Scriptures state that every regenerated person has the Holy Spirit living in him. What is his further need? He needs to be baptized or filled with the Holy Spirit, for while all Christians *have* the Holy Spirit, not all Christians are *filled* with the Spirit.

What is the condition of the regenerated person as he lives in this world without being filled with the Spirit? There are some things of which he is sure. For one, he is a new creature in Christ. He knows that his life has been changed through the work and presence of the Holy Spirit. In this relationship he knows he is a child of God. But there are times when he is aware of the active presence of something within that is contrary to this new life, and to the nature and will of God. It is something related to the fact that man is born in sin. So a conflict exists.

There are some scriptures which describe this condition within the lives of Christians—a condition which is called "carnal." For example, the Corinthian people to whom Paul wrote were Christians, as the greetings of Paul in his first letter to them would indicate (see 1:1-6). But in a later statement Paul says to them:

> *And I, brethren, could not speak unto you as unto spiritual, but as unto carnal, even as unto babes in Christ. I have fed you with milk, and not with meat: for hitherto ye were not able to bear it, neither yet now are ye able. For ye are yet carnal: for whereas there is among you envying, and strife, and divisions, are ye not carnal, and walk as men? For while one saith, I am of Paul; and another, I am of Apollos; are ye not carnal?* (1 Cor. 3:1-4).

Yet at the same time Paul says: "Know ye not that ye are the temple of God, and that the Spirit of God dwelleth in you?" (3:16). If, as some teachers think, this statement refers to the Church as the temple of the Spirit of God, Paul makes another statement which stresses the individual aspect: "Know ye not that your body is the temple of the Holy Spirit which is in you, which ye have of God?" (6:19).

This question may be raised: Will the Holy Spirit dwell in a carnal heart? Evidently these scriptures say that He will. John Wesley raises and answers this question: "But could they be unholy, while they were the temples of the Holy Ghost? Yes; that they were temples of the Holy Ghost is certain, and it is equally certain, they were, in some degree, carnal, that is unholy" (sermon, "Sin in Believers").

The Scriptures teach, and it is verified in human experience, that while the Holy Spirit abides in the regenerate person there is at times a condition of internal strife existing, which Paul describes as follows: "For the flesh [carnal] lusteth [wars] against the Spirit, and the Spirit against the flesh: and these are contrary the one to the other: so that ye cannot do the things that ye would" (Gal. 5:17).

John Wesley's comment on this verse is helpful:

> The apostle here directly affirms that the flesh, evil nature, opposes the Spirit, even in believers; that even in the regenerate, there are two principles, "contrary the one to the other." . . . A man may have the Spirit of God dwelling in him, and may walk after the Spirit, though he still feels "the flesh lusting against the Spirit" (sermon, "Sin in Believers").

There seems to be no reason to believe that this is a constant condition of life or that it is the norm of the regenerated life. There are many times when there are manifestations of the Spirit in victories over those things which would defeat, but at other times there may be manifestations of a carnal disposition. At times the conflict may be strong; at other times it is not. But whatever are the manifestations of this condition of life, we know it is not satisfying to God nor to the Christian. God has something better for His people; they may be filled with the Spirit or sanctified wholly.

Let us consider this condition from another approach. The basic factor of the human individual is the presence of many instincts and impulses—innate desires which the person directs toward the desired ends of his life. These many instincts may be classified under three areas: self, sex, and society. These instincts are basic factors of life which cannot be destroyed. They remain in the person throughout his life and direct his interests and behavior tendencies. But these instincts can be redirected to a new center of life, for they are themselves neither good nor bad. They may be directed toward good ends or they may be directed toward bad ends. The responsible person does the directing.

When Paul speaks of "the flesh," he means a life in which these natural instincts and impulses have been wrongly directed—perverted toward the ends of sin. This is why Paul speaks of "sin in the flesh," making a distinction between sin and the flesh, for in this manner "the flesh" means the instincts and drives of the person directed toward sin. To "live in the flesh" is to live on the level of the instincts. The result of living on the level of the instincts is what Paul calls "the works of the flesh." These "works" are found in four different areas: *sensuality* —"immoral, filthy, and indecent actions"; *wrong religious practices*—"in worship of idols and witchcraft ("magic," is the Moffatt translation); *loveless actions and dispositional evils*—"People become enemies, they fight, become jealous ['murder,' KJV], angry, and ambitious. They separate into parties and groups; they are envious"; *intemperance*—"get drunk, have orgies" (Gal. 5:19-21, TEV). This is why Paul says the carnal mind or the flesh is enmity against God (Rom. 8:7).

In the sinful life there is a dominant center of life in which the instincts are directed toward the ends of sin and self. The person is restrained in his conduct, however, by his own character ideals and those of society, and further by his responses to the prevenient grace of God. But, in general, the flesh is the ruling power of his life. As a result, he has one center of life with few conflicts.

With the coming of the Holy Spirit into his life in the work of regeneration, a person is given a new center of life, new reasons for living. His instinctive drives and interests are now directed toward this new center, Christ, who is made real to him through the indwelling Holy Spirit. But the old way of living in the flesh, the old behavior tendencies, although they are greatly changed, are not completely directed and organized into the new ends of life. Hence the conflict exists which Paul described in the words: "For the desires of the flesh are against the Spirit, and the desires of the Spirit are against the flesh; for these are opposed to each other, to prevent you from doing what you would" (Gal. 5:17, RSV). Which means that instead of there being one center of life, there are now two centers. Life revolves around them in a sort of ellipse, the focus at one end being the Spirit and at the other the flesh, with the Spirit being by far the more powerful.

Let us take a close look at this conflict. First, it says, "The flesh [carnal] lusteth against the Spirit, and the Spirit against the flesh, and these are contrary the one to the other." There is an inner conflict. Second, it indicates a deprived state: "So that you cannot do the things that ye would," or, "So that what you will to do you cannot" (NEB). One thing we should always keep in mind is that the conflict is not on equal terms. The balance of victory is always on the side of the Spirit, although there may be an occasional defeat because the flesh sometimes prevails.

This condition of conflict presents a real problem. It is true that every Christian desires to give undivided loyalty to Christ, but at the same time he may feel a pull toward the old self with its desires which are contrary to the desires inspired by the Holy Spirit within him. Every Christian wishes to love God with all the heart, soul, mind, and strength; but he is hindered by the conflict between this desire and self-love, or the love of the world, or the love for something that is outside the will of God for him.

On the other hand, the Christian is inspired by the indwelling Spirit to do acts of sacrificial service for Christ, but the carnal self is in conflict with this. In this case, the conflict may come from fear of others, or fear of failure, or the love of ease which shrinks from the sacrifice. There are many other manifestations of the conflict too numerous to mention. But the statement we are considering that "subsequent to this there is the deeper work of heart cleansing or entire sanctification through the infilling of the Holy Spirit" stresses the fact that such a state of conflict is not the best experience God has for the Christian. The conflict can be resolved through the baptism or filling with the Holy Spirit, or His further work of heart cleansing.

We have noted that in Paul's statement a deprived state also exists, "So that ye cannot do the things that ye would." There are people who interpret this statement to mean what I heard a man say recently: "I know I am a Christian, but I do every day those things I ought not to do, and I leave undone those things which I ought to do. Pray for me, that I may be faithful." But Paul did not say that. Such a life is not the true Christian life, for the child of God has dominion over sins both of commission and of omission (cf. Rom. 6:14). What Paul means is that the Christian is deprived. Because of the inner conflict he is unable to be the joyous, wholehearted, victorious person the Spirit inspires him to be. His spiritual vitality is sapped. So much of his effort, prayer, and energy is directed toward his overcoming in the conflict that at times he cannot give to Christ the full and loving service he desires to give Him. There are situations when he wants to be courageous in his stand for Christ but he fails to take his stand and is defeated, weakened by the conflict within. There are times in temptation when he is betrayed by the flesh and is overcome. His witness for Christ may not be as effective as he desires it to be because of this deprived state.

No Christian can live permanently in such a state of conflict and weakness. The conflict will have to be resolved one way or another. The person may almost unconsciously drift to the flesh in taking the way of least resistance. He may not go back into former sins, but he continues to live a religious life on the basis of the human, continuing to follow the religious habits formed when the Spirit directed his life. But his life is void of a spiritual dynamic; it is now a religious routine without joy, or blessing, or the consciousness of the presence of God. What a tragedy! The conflict is gone but it is because he has yielded to the flesh. On the other hand, the conflict may be resolved by yielding fully to the Holy Spirit, by making a full and total commitment of himself to God and being filled with and empowered by the Holy Spirit. What a life that can be!

The desire and purpose of God for His children is to bring them unity and harmony at the center of life with the inner conflict between the flesh and the Spirit resolved and with the human instincts and impulses directed toward Christ in a Spirit-filled or sanctified life. It is a unity in relationship with Christ through the Spirit.

The testimony of the Apostle Paul is, "The law of the Spirit of life in Christ Jesus hath made me free from the law of sin and death" (Rom. 8:2). He seems here to relate this "law of sin and death" to "the flesh." McKenzie says,

> To be free from "the law of sin and death" is to be free from the law of sinful habit, sinful dispositions, sinful attitude of mind; free not because the mind has been emptied of its instinctive tendencies or capacity to acquire desires, but because these have found new end-motives in harmony with the mind of Christ. The behavior-tendencies become linked with the spiritual ends of the soul, or the spiritual personality.[1]

Bishop R. S. Foster, a leader in the holiness movement at the beginning of this century, states these facts of experience from a different angle:

> It [fallen human nature] has no new wrong element, but the elements are wrongly adjusted. Now if it were abandoned to itself its debauchment would be utter

and inconceivable; but it is not. The powers are still there; they have only been disordered, playing wrong and ineffective parts. Conscience is still there, and reason, but they are enslaved; they remonstrate, but they cannot rule; they cannot be hushed, but they are not respected. What is needed is that right order should be restored.[2]

He affirms that in the work of the Holy Spirit in entire sanctification the full order is restored and that which is abnormal in man becomes normal, with the disordered faculties brought into a state of order when "a new controlling and regulating life manifests itself. . . . The new life awakened is a life of supreme love to God and right, and its expression is worship and obedience."[3]

Paul has another way of describing this deliverance from the flesh: "They that are Christ's have crucified the flesh with the affections and lusts," or, as Barclay translates it, "Those who belong to Christ Jesus have once and for all crucified their lower nature (flesh) with its passions and desires" (Gal. 5:24). This is a symbolic way of saying that life, with its instincts and impulses directed toward sin, with its passions and desires, has been definitely brought to an end, and that life is organized around a new center, Christ Jesus. In other words, it means to die indeed unto sin in order to be alive unto God (Rom. 6:11). This corresponds with another statement of testimony made by Paul: "I am crucified with Christ: nevertheless I live; yet not I, but Christ liveth in me: and the life which I now live in the flesh [body] I live by the faith of the Son of God, who loved me, and gave himself for me" (Gal. 2:20).

The essential human instincts are not crucified; rather the whole order of life has been changed by the Holy Spirit. The instincts are now directed to new end-motives of following Christ in a Spirit-filled life and without reserve to activities and service in a relation with Him which glorifies God.

The provision God has made for this integrated life in a relationship with the Spirit is twofold: (1) The crucifixion of self. "Wherefore Jesus also, that he might sanctify the people with his own blood, suffered without the gate. Let us go forth therefore unto him without the camp, bearing his reproach" (Heb. 13:12-13). (2) The fullness or baptism with the Holy Spirit. Let us then look at this work of God as He brings man who is born in sin into the relationship with himself in heart cleansing.

Filled with the Holy Spirit

This is the experience which the followers of Jesus received on the Day of Pentecost when they were all filled with the Holy Ghost (Acts 2:4). In that experience, according to the testimony of Peter, their hearts were purified by faith (Acts 15:9). The fullness of the Spirit expelled all impurities from their hearts. It brought to them a wholeness and peace which resolved the inner conflict until with singleness of heart and purpose they loved and served God with their instincts fully directed toward that end. This was not only a personal experience in the lives of these people; it also brought them into a personal relationship with God, the Holy Spirit, and with each other in the Church, the body of believers.

The comparison in the lives of these followers of Jesus between what they were before this experience of Pentecost and after they were filled with the Holy Spirit is a pattern of what we, at least in some measure, may expect in our lives after being filled with the Spirit.

1. *They were filled with the Spirit to the exclusion of all foreign elements.* Selfishness was removed; they each sought no more the chief places nor was there any more arguing about who would be the greatest in the Kingdom. They now were of "one heart and one soul" (Acts 4:32);

they gave themselves to God and to each other without reservation. They were filled with the love of God; each gave himself in self-forgetting service to Christ and to others. They were more ambitious for the spread of the kingdom of God than for anything else, and they preached the gospel of Christ everywhere, even when it meant great sacrifice and suffering to themselves.

2. *They were filled with the Holy Spirit in the sense that they were possessed of a master passion.* They gave themselves fully to Christ in everyday life. Their human vacillations were gone and they burned with a holy passion to serve Christ in the ministry of the Word. They were possessed of an enthusiasm, a zeal, which nothing, not even death, could quench. They had a holy boldness which made them fearless in the presence of their greatest foes. They faced every attack of the evil one with courage and in the confidence that in their relationship with God they would have victory. They were conscious of a divine mission and they were impelled by the love of Christ and the fire of the Holy Spirit to fulfill it. Nothing could stop them.

3. *They were filled with the Holy Spirit, which brought to them a sense of adequacy.* They were enabled to meet whatever life brought to them with a poise not natural to them. It was a poise and confidence born of their relationship with the Spirit. They were so filled with the Spirit that they began to give spontaneous utterance to the wonderful works of God. This expression from overflowing hearts broke the conventional bounds, for the people heard them speak in the languages in which they were born. There was an awareness of power. God spoke and worked through them to move people to recognize the truth of their message and to accept Christ as Saviour and Messiah. The fullness of the Spirit within them fulfilled the promise of Jesus that from within them would flow "rivers of living

water" (John 7:38). This flowing out of the Spirit was greater than the outside pressures of life, so they lived victoriously.

4. *There was an awareness of the presence of the living Christ.* This was made real to them by the Holy Spirit —God in the present tense—whose mission it is to testify of Jesus (John 16:14-15). It was "with great power [that] the apostles gave their testimony to the resurrection of the Lord Jesus" (Acts 4:33, RSV). They never thought of Jesus as only having lived, He was much more alive to them than a figure of history. They were living in a vital relationship with Him; He was their living Companion. His presence made them resurrected persons, persons who lived in the power of His resurrection. It was this consciousness of Jesus' presence that inspired their fellowship and made them invincible. He was the Source of their joy and victory in the midst of some fierce persecutions. Jesus Christ was so alive, so real to them that they became known as "Christians"—people who belong to Christ. This reality of the presence of the living Christ in daily life is characteristic of Spirit-filled people today.

The encouraging word for us is that we, too, *may be filled with the Holy Spirit—NOW.* The inner conflict between the flesh and the Spirit within us can be brought to an end *now.* We can *now* experience that cleansing of heart and fullness of life. We can know that possession of a master passion until our lives will be devoted *now* to the doing of the things God wants done in our world. We can have that sense of adequacy, of power, of poise that only the fullness of the Spirit can give—and He can give it to us *now.* God desires His people today to be persons filled with the Spirit, that they may manifest to the world the results of such a filling. How important it is that we *now* receive the Spirit in His fullness!

This is how God works with man, who is born in sin,

to bring him to the experience of being filled with the Holy Spirit, or being sanctified wholly. He works with man through His prevenient grace from the earliest days of his life. Through the work of the Spirit in regeneration, when man repents and receives Christ as Saviour, He enables him to live in this world a righteous life. And through the further work of the Holy Spirit in sanctifying grace, He cleanses his heart and fills him with himself. Through this climactic relationship with Him comes an adequacy and power to live in this world a life which is devoted to God and which brings blessing to his associates.

Some Spiritual Disciplines

The Spirit-filled life is made more fruitful and satisfying when we as responsible Christians observe the necessary disciplines of such a life. This means that we are consciously directing our total selfhood—our instincts, our impulses, drives, etc.—toward the end of living to glorify God. Our goal is to be conformed to the image of God's dear Son (Rom. 8:29).

One phase of these disciplines has to do with our instincts, of which Paul wrote:

So then, my brothers, you can see that we have no particular reason . . . to live life on the level of the instincts. Indeed that way of living leads to certain spiritual death. But if on the other hand you cut the nerve of your instinctive actions by obeying the Spirit, you are on the way to real living (Rom. 8:12-13, Phillips).

All temptations to live on the level of the instincts must be put to death, or overcome, through obeying the Spirit, or through having a vital relationship with Him.

This is equal to what Paul said of himself: "I keep under my body." Barclay translates this, "I batter my body; I make it realize that I am its master, for I do not want to preach to others, and then to find that I myself have failed to stand the test" (1 Cor. 9:27).

It is to our interest to note that this discipline is accomplished by or through the Spirit—God in the present tense. It is not done solely in our own strength; it is through our working with Him.

The same thought of discipline was mentioned by Paul in his letter to the Thessalonians when he said that, through being sanctified, "every one of you should learn to control his body, keeping it pure and treating it with respect, and never regarding it as an instrument for self-gratification, as do pagans with no knowledge of God" 1 Thess. 4:4-5, Phillips).

There is another area to this discipline: "Walk in the Spirit, and ye shall not fulfil the lust of the flesh" (Gal. 5:16). Here is required a continuous, persistent action—to *walk* in the Spirit. Phillips puts it, "Live your whole life in the Spirit." That is, by the help of the Spirit direct your instincts toward the end of living your whole life in Him. This is the secret of living a sanctified life in this world and in a body whose instincts were formerly directed toward the ends of sin. Through the fullness of the Spirit, the change has been so complete that the flesh has been crucified with its passions and desires until there is a life of victory through Christ. The total person is directed toward the end of glorifying Him in this world.

Sometimes we strive to make a distinction between what is carnal and what is human in the Christian life, but this is a futile and useless endeavor. Our concern should be to fully walk in the Spirit and by His help be normal Christian persons with the instincts and impulses directed toward that end. When we are absorbed in this way of living, we desire only to walk in the Spirit and to manifest more and more "the fruit of the Spirit [which] is love, joy, peace, patience, kindness, goodness, faithfulness, gentleness, self-control" (Gal. 5:22-23, RSV).

Chapter
TWO

Sanctified by the Holy Spirit

Entire sanctification is a teaching of the Scriptures, a personal experience in human life, and a doctrine of the Christian Church. In this sequence the doctrine comes last because it is a united human effort to describe or explain in language the spiritual experience wrought by the Holy Spirit in a person who believes the teachings of the Scriptures. A doctrinal statement is important, for it provides a basis for unity of thought within the church. It is a rallying point for the church's thinking, for its activities and for its outreach in the world. So there is no better place to begin our thinking about the teachings of the church on entire sanctification than with the creed of our church stated in its *Manual*. For the purpose of this discussion we will rearrange the statement slightly, making it to read:

> Through the baptism with the Holy Spirit, which is an act of God subsequent to regeneration, believers are entirely sanctified; and are brought into a state of entire devotement to God, and the holy obedience of love made perfect (adapted from the *Manual*, 1972, p. 31).

The advantage of this arrangement is that we begin with a Person who does the work instead of with an experience; then we proceed to think of the work He does in persons. This may help us to understand that the experience of entire sanctification is the result of a certain personal relationship with a divine Person, for we are sanctified by the Holy Spirit (Rom. 15:16).

This tells us that entire sanctification is not an abstract experience; rather it is a Person, the Holy Spirit, coming in His fullness into us as persons, cleansing our hearts from sin and empowering us for life and service in our world. One person described this experience in relationship as "the invasion of my person and life by the Holy Spirit, who in His coming gave me a sense of purity and a deeper relation with Christ."

Our first consideration, therefore, is the medium through which we are brought into the experience of entire sanctification and the glorious, rewarding relationship with the living Christ.

The Baptism with the Holy Spirit

Since we have already stated the doctrine, that it is through the baptism with the Holy Spirit we are entirely sanctified, let us look at some of its scriptural background. We begin with John the Baptist, who in speaking of the coming of Jesus said:

> *I indeed baptize you with water unto repentance: but he that cometh after me is mightier than I, whose shoes I am not worthy to bear: he shall baptize with the Holy Ghost, and with fire: whose fan is in his hand, and he will throughly purge his floor, and gather the wheat into the garner; but he will burn up the chaff with unquenchable fire* (Matt. 3:11-12).

The risen Christ in His conversations with His disciples before His ascension

> *commanded them that they should not depart from Jerusalem, but wait for the promise of the Father, which, saith he, ye have heard of me. For John truly baptized with water; but ye shall be baptized with the Holy Ghost not many days hence. . . . Ye shall receive power, after that the Holy Ghost is come upon you: and ye shall be witnesses unto me* (Acts 1:4-5, 8).

Those "not many days hence" passed and the fulfillment of that promise of Jesus came, as described by Luke: "And when the day of Pentecost was fully come, they were all with one accord in one place. . . . And they were all filled with the Holy Ghost" (Acts 2:1, 4).

It is of interest for us to note the use of two words in these statements; they are the words "baptized" and "filled." The statement of promise was, "Ye shall be *baptized* with the Holy Ghost" (1:5); the statement of fulfillment was, "They were all *filled* with the Holy Ghost" (2:4, italics mine). The two words are used interchangeably, which means that to be baptized with the Holy Ghost is to be filled with the Holy Ghost, or to be filled with the Holy Ghost is to be baptized with the Holy Ghost; and to be baptized or filled with the Holy Ghost is to be entirely sanctified, for this is the result of His coming in His fullness into human life.

The Apostle Peter was used of God to take the message of Christ to the Gentiles in the home of Cornelius, the Roman centurion in Caesarea. As Peter was speaking to them, "the Holy Ghost fell on all them which heard the word" (Acts 10:44). In commenting on this occasion to the heads of the Jerusalem Church, Peter said:

> *And as I began to speak, the Holy Ghost fell on them, as on us at the beginning [i.e., on the Day of Pentecost]. Then remembered I the word of the Lord, how that he said, John indeed baptized with water; but ye shall be baptized with the Holy Ghost* (Acts 11:15-16).

Later in his testimony before the church council which was considering the status of the Gentiles in the Christian faith, Peter said:

> *Men and brethren, ye know how that a good while ago God made choice among us, that the Gentiles by my mouth should hear the word of the gospel, and believe [referring to his experience at the home of Cornelius]. And God, which knoweth the hearts, bare them [the Gentiles] witness, giving them the Holy Ghost, even as he did unto us [Jews at Pentecost]; and put no difference between us [Jews] and them [Gentiles], purifying their hearts by faith* (Acts 15:7-9).

This testimony of Peter tells us several facts. First, that the disciples and others were filled with the Holy Spirit on the Day of Pentecost (Acts 2:4), and that in His filling them He purified their hearts by faith. Second, that the Holy Spirit fell upon the Gentile believers at the house of Cornelius (Acts 10:34-48; 11:15-16), and in His falling upon them their hearts were purified by faith. The emphasis is upon the Person, the Holy Spirit, who did in persons the work of "purifying their hearts by faith."

What does this say to us? It tells us that we can have pure hearts and be spiritually dynamic. We can live clean and useful lives in our world. In our lives as Christians we can enjoy something vitally alive, something that is real, something that testifies of Christ without our saying much. All this comes only through the active presence and fullness of the Holy Spirit, a Person, who in a relationship with us sanctifies and keeps us as His own possession.

In the message of the Acts of the Apostles there are many references made to the baptism or filling with the Holy Spirit. Some of them stress an epochal spiritual experience for those who are Christian believers, while others emphasize the continuing fullness of the Spirit in the lives of persons who have had an epochal experience and are living in a relationship with the Holy Spirit. Such an experience seems to be related to the Church as a whole. The references are: "They were all filled with the Holy Ghost" (2:4; 4:31); the first deacons were men who were filled with the Holy Ghost (6:5); the apostles Peter and John went to Samaria, that the converts from the revival led by Philip "might receive the Holy Ghost" (8:15); Ananias' ministry to Saul of Tarsus was "that thou mightest receive thy sight, and be filled with the Holy Ghost" (9:17); Peter preached to the Gentiles at the home of Cornelius and as he preached "the Holy Ghost fell on them" (10:44); in giving an account of this incident Peter related it to the baptism with the Holy Ghost (11:14); Paul inquired of the disciples he found at Ephesus, "Have ye received the Holy Ghost since ye believed?" (19:2).

In one place in the Acts of the Apostles, purity of heart by faith, or what we think of as entire sanctification, is related to the baptism with the Holy Spirit. It is in connection with the incident already referred to in which Peter spoke before the church council (15:7-9).

The fullness of the Holy Spirit was something very vital in the life and activities of the early Christian Church. They were indeed people of the Spirit. When we think of the baptism with the Holy Spirit, we think of God filling our hearts and lives with himself. We think of His cleansing our hearts from sin and enabling us through a living relationship with Him to be and to do what would otherwise be impossible. We become people of the Spirit. He indeed is the One who sanctifies us wholly, for we are "sanctified by the Holy Ghost."

Will you believe it? The triune God is with you in the here and now. In this relationship with Him, He is helping you now just where you need that help most. He is giving you insights of what He can do for and with you, assuring you that He is ready now to fill you with the Holy Spirit, or sanctify you wholly. Not only that; He will keep you sanctified in this world in which you live. This means that you will then enjoy a relationship with the Spirit, a relationship which will qualify you as a witness for Christ and equip you to do whatever service He is asking you to do. Think of what a change He can make in you now if in this relationship you will permit Him to work within you and with you in ways that He desires, and will walk in obedience to Him.

This living in relationship with the Holy Spirit, who is sanctifying you wholly now, is a very important fact of reality. It is not something far out; it is something that is very vital in your living now. The Holy Spirit is doing something for and with you now, something which He keeps on doing as you respond to Him in this relationship. As you walk in fellowship and obedience with Christ who is made real to you by the Spirit's presence, He accomplishes His will in your life.

The Person Is All-important

The third part of our opening statement was that entire sanctification is a personal experience in human life. This makes the person in his relationship with the Divine Person all-important.

There is a rather general custom in religious circles to talk more about the action of God than about God himself.

For example, I heard a person in a rather joyous mood say, "I thank God for the plan of salvation." Why was he thankful for a "plan," a thing, when he could have praised and thanked the Saviour, a Person, for His personal work of salvation in his life? Why do we hear people say, "I thank God for sanctification," instead of being thankful for the Person by whom the provision was made and who is the One who sanctifies? We seem to forget the Person in the enjoyment of His gifts.

Sometimes we substitute theological terms for the Person. We have put labels on God's acts in salvation, such as justification, regeneration, sanctification, etc. It is not infrequently that we present these labels to people instead of exalting the Person whose works these labels describe. These technical, theological terms have a rightful place; and when they are used by good and wise teachers, they explain the workings of God in the lives of people. But these terms and explanations are no substitute for Christ, the Saviour. He is the One who loves each of us with undying love, the One who in His love for us died and rose again that He might bring us to God. He is the One who has so lovingly followed us in our lives to draw us to himself, that indeed He might change us by forgiving our sins and making us new persons. And He is the One who, in His love, leads us in a developing relationship with Him to be filled with the Holy Spirit or to be sanctified wholly. What a mistake to substitute something He *does* for a Saviour like Christ *is!*

In the description of the work of Christ, you will note that though we have spoken of the Spirit's work in us and referred to these theological terms, we have emphasized the *Person,* Christ, the Saviour, who does the work in a personal relationship with us. Indeed the Person is all-important, and the persons who have experienced His work are important. There is a personal relationship here which no act, no thing, no doctrine, no term can replace.

This points up something very important in the experience of entire sanctification. Some people say, "I can't understand the doctrine of entire sanctification." Sometimes this failure to understand exists because there is no desire to understand. But many who make the statement are sincere. It could be that the professors of the experience of entire sanctification are to blame because of the way in which they have tried to explain the doctrine. They have begun with an experience, something which has happened to them, instead of beginning with a Person, the Holy Spirit, who has brought them into this experience and life. They have endeavored to explain what happens, why one needs it, and what one must do to keep it. All of this has a place; but they have failed to tell of the Holy Spirit, God in the present tense, who in a very personal way has been working with them. He has brought them into a fullness of relationship with himself, has filled them and sanctified them wholly.

We should always stress that sanctification is part of a growing relationship with a Person; One who is worthy of receiving our lives, our love, our total person; One who leads on into a deeper relationship with Him through the experience of entire sanctification or the baptism with the Holy Spirit. It is an experience in personal relationship that needs to be explained.

The plain fact is, *we can love an experience but an experience cannot love us.* We need ever to love Christ with the whole heart, love Him because He is a living reality in our lives through the presence of the Holy Spirit, love Him because we know that He first loved us, and love Him because this is what we desire to do more than anything else. This is what sanctification really is—the work of the Holy Spirit, who has brought us into a place where we can love

Christ with all our hearts in a continuing personal relationship while we live in our sinful world.

The analogy to marriage may give us a better understanding of what we mean. What answer would you give to the question, "What do you mean by marriage?" You might say: "Marriage is something which takes place when two persons of the opposite sex decide to unite in matrimony and live their lives together." Then to elaborate, you might add: "In this act of marriage each of them gives up the privilege of going out with persons of the opposite sex. They separate themselves from their parents and take upon themselves new responsibilities and work. They change their ways of living and thinking and perhaps do without many of the things to which they were accustomed before marriage. They are now governed largely by the customary thinking and activities of married people. They are just married; that's about all you can say."

There is much truth in such a statement. But this is not a true description of marriage, for it contains many misconceptions about the wedded life.

The statement overlooks the fact that marriage begins with love and that the marriage itself is the product of love. Marriage is the union of two persons whose desire for each other has developed through a personal relationship of deepening love. They ultimately decide to enter into this deeper relationship of marriage. The relationship began when the two people met and found a strong mutual attraction. As they became better acquainted, love developed in each heart. In time they became engaged and pledged their love for each other as a continuing experience.

This engagement is an important step in the development of their relationship. It makes a difference in their thinking and planning for the future. But it is not marriage. A second important step is necessary to seal that bond. In a wedding ceremony they are brought together, and a union of love which already exists is publicly acknowledged and certified in marriage. They so love each other that they are now one. Because of that love they are willing to pay whatever the cost may be to make their marriage a fulfilling and satisfying life to both. This personal relationship in love is what counts.

Too often we try to explain to some sincere person what sanctification means on somewhat the same basis that marriage was explained above, in which the personal relationship of love was hardly mentioned. It is vitally necessary to keep in mind that the person is all-important in all of God's working with mankind.

This analogy of marriage pictures quite well what entire sanctification means. The process of development is much the same. We become acquainted with Jesus Christ and recognize His love for us. We respond to His love by giving our hearts and lives to Him, and in His love He accepts us through forgiving our sins and making us new persons. We continue to develop our relationship with our Saviour, and our love for Him increases. Eventually we recognize that we can deepen this relationship by giving ourselves fully to Him as a love-gift of our total selves. This demands a full consecration, that indeed He may have us as His very own.

Our trust in Him assures us that He accepts us in a deeper sense than ever before and He gives to us the fullness of the Holy Spirit, who sanctifies us wholly. This is a most wonderful personal experience, but it is more than an experience. It is a relationship between persons, the blessed Saviour and ourselves, which brings an entirely new joy in fellowship and a new feeling of adequacy for life through the presence of the Holy Spirit. So we mean by entire sanctification a real and vital personal relationship with Christ through the Holy Spirit, or being baptized with the Holy Spirit. In His abiding presence He makes the living Christ more and more real to us in fellowship and life.

If we spend our energies merely trying to keep an experience, it will be a futile effort. But if we give ourselves to maintaining a living relationship with Christ, it will be a wonderful and rewarding way of living. For entire sanctification is experienced through a developing relationship with a Person, and the life of holiness is lived through trust and obedience.

God Is at Work in Us

The kind of relationship we enjoy with God is implied in the words: "Work out your own salvation with fear and trembling ['awe and reverence,' Phillips]. For it is God which worketh in you both to will and to do of his good pleasure" (Phil. 2:12-13).

In this wonderful relationship we work *out* what God is working *in* us in the process of salvation. We are prone to think of the experience of entire sanctification as something abstract, something we either have or we don't have. We overlook the fact that such an experience is brought to us through God working in us and it is maintained as we cooperate with Him or "work out" what He is working in us.

An evangelist took for the text of his sermon, "Have ye received the Holy Ghost since ye believed?" (Acts 19:2). After reading his text he immediately turned his thought to sanctification, making the text to read, "Have you been sanctified since you were justified?" He preached a good sermon, but his interpretation was not accurate. He put spiritual experiences in the place of a Person. The text said, "Have ye received the Holy Ghost?" not, "Have you been sanctified?" He mentioned the Holy Spirit only once or twice in his sermon; the Person was hidden under the work He does.

At times the teachings of Jesus suffer the same misinterpretation. Jesus stressed the coming of the Comforter, the Holy Spirit, as the Bringer of great benefits to His people. Only twice did He talk about sanctification (cf. John 17:17, 19), but many times did He stress the importance of the coming of the Comforter, the Holy Spirit—a Person—into the lives of His people and into the world. He said when He (the Comforter) came He would lead or guide them into all truth, He would teach them and make known to them the things of Christ. He would reveal Christ himself and would recall to their minds the things He had said to them. He would also empower them for life and service. It was the coming of a Person, the Comforter, the Holy Spirit, that He stressed more than the subjective experience He would bring to believers. He is indeed the Sanctifier, but how wrong it is to put the experience as the point of emphasis rather than the Person who does the work!

The post-resurrection ministry of Jesus makes this same emphasis. He commanded His disciples not to depart from Jerusalem until the promise of the Father—the Holy Spirit—had come upon them—not until they were sanctified (Acts 1:4). He promised them, "Ye shall receive power," but it would be "after that the Holy Ghost is come upon you" (Acts 1:8). His emphasis was on a positive factor, the coming of a Person, the Holy Spirit, not on purity, although He knew that purity of heart would result from His coming.

Let us return to the analogy of marriage. Here is a young man who has been married a few years and is enthusiastic about this institution of marriage. He tells in glowing terms how wonderful it is to have a home, to enjoy its comforts, to have satisfying meals prepared for him, to have his clothes kept clean and in good repair, etc. A child has been born and he exults in the joys and honor of fatherhood. He affirms that all young men ought to get married and experience such joys.

But suppose that in all his praise of marriage and home life and fatherhood he, perhaps unconsciously, never mentions his wife, the very one who has made possible the blessings he has extolled. He has thoughtlessly failed to recognize that marriage is more than an institution; it is a deep personal relationship between two persons who have devoted themselves to each other. What an oversight!

In the same way we may be guilty of a thoughtless attitude toward the Holy Spirit, the Sanctifier. We extol His work. ("Oh, it is wonderful to be sanctified!"; "Every Christian should enter into the joys of being entirely sanctified"; etc.) But we overlook the most important factor —the Person who sanctifies. It is the Holy Spirit who sanctifies; it is He who is the Source and Giver of the blessings and victories of the sanctified life. It is He who baptizes, who fills, who makes Christ real to us, and makes available to us all that Christ has provided in His life, death, and resurrection. This includes, of course, the cleansing of our hearts through His blood, or our being entirely sanctified. But it is the presence of the Holy Spirit working in us that makes the Spirit-filled life so wonderful.

Much of the "nominal living" among professing holiness people is the result of this faulty emphasis. We are striving to keep an experience instead of maintaining a joyful relationship with Christ through the Spirit. We will never know the full joys of fellowship with the living Christ, the true satisfaction of living a sanctified life, or the thrill of making Him known to other people until we get our emphasis straight. These are realized, not by "watching an experience," but by working out in a growing relationship with Christ what He is working in our lives.

Through this fellowship in the Spirit we are able to live a sanctified life in our world.

ONE LIFE: TWO EXPERIENCES

A person is a unit, so whatever God does for him involves the entire person. Salvation is the work of God which involves a lifetime process. There is a past tense to salvation when, through the grace of God, our sins are forgiven and we are made the children of God. But salvation in its fullest sense also includes the further work of the Spirit in heart cleansing.

There is a present tense to salvation in that, in a way, we are always being saved by the grace of God—in the hour of test and temptation, in the midst of life's severest experiences, and in other such problems and pressures. In these, salvation means that in our continuing relation with God He goes through them all with us. He assures us by His presence and love of His saving, healing, comforting, inspiring, and strengthening power. His strong arm upholds us. It is salvation in that we are "kept by the power of God through faith" (1 Pet. 1:5).

But there is also a future tense in salvation—"salvation ready to be revealed in the last time," which means eternal life in the presence of our glorified Saviour, Christ Jesus. In all of these phases of salvation it is the one person who, in relationship with Christ, experiences them. There are not three different salvations; it is salvation in a continuing process in which God brings us from persons born in sin to those who are finally redeemed in eternity with Christ.

There have been some unwholesome interpretations of these spiritual experiences the person passes through in the process of salvation. Some have taught that the work of the Spirit in regeneration or the new birth and His further work of entire sanctification are not only two different works of grace but they must always be kept separate and distinct in life.

For example, one teacher insisted that in God's work of regeneration we receive the love of God, and in His further work of entire sanctification we receive perfect love, but that the two loves are not related to each other. The Scriptures do teach that "the love of God is shed abroad in our hearts" in justification (Rom. 5:1, 5); but perfect love is not the gift of another kind of love, for it is said "our love [is] made perfect" (1 John 4:17). A love already possessed through our relationship with the Holy Spirit is made perfect. Further we read: "Whoso keepeth his word, in him verily is the love of God perfected" (1 John 2:5); and, "If we love one another, God dwelleth in us, and his love is perfected in us" (1 John 4:12). The perfecting in love is a further step in the process of God's working with us in salvation, a step in which the total person is involved.

Another teacher has strongly insisted that John Wesley was wrong in his teaching that sanctification is begun in regeneration, and "the second work of grace properly so called" (Wesley) is the work of God in entire sanctification. This teacher's interpretation seemed to be that these two spiritual experiences are unrelated. One follows the other, he said, and they must be kept separate and distinct. He failed to recognize the correctness of Wesley's teaching in that, while one followed the other in time, they were but two different steps in God's working with man. In the process of salvation, the person is brought toward the fulfillment of God's destiny for him, and is being conformed to the image of Christ (Rom. 8:29).

This error crops up in various ways. For example, a person said recently, "I lost my sanctification, but I did not lose my regeneration." As if to say, "I lost one of my spiritual appendages, but I kept the other." We must recognize that the work of the Holy Spirit in our lives is not something added to our persons in some mystical manner. These wonderful experiences are not appendages at all but vital experiences with God working in us in the process of salvation.

To be sure, some radical changes are made in the person himself. He experiences forgiveness of sins and a change takes place within him which can be described by no better figure than being "born again." But this is not a new nature added to him; he himself has been changed. He sustains a new relationship with God; he is His child. The alienation which sin had brought is gone; there is full reconciliation with God and the Spirit of Christ dwells within him (Rom. 8:9). He now shares a life in the Spirit with all other persons in the body of Christ who are thus related to God. He enjoys the "communion of saints" and shares in doing the work of Christ in this world.

In this new relationship with the Holy Spirit he is conscious not only of new life but also of new and great resources made available to him by the Spirit. Through the Spirit he obeys God in a spontaneous response of love for Christ. He is no longer a slave of sinful habits, attitudes, and dispositions; for through the power and guidance of the Spirit he has a growing understanding of what the Christian life should be and can be. The new has come to him and the old is gone. He has new reasons for living. Christ has become the focal point of his life and he earnestly desires that the whole of his life as a person be centered in Him. He is concerned for and actively works with other people in seeking to win them to Christ, who can meet their needs too.

Whatever life in the future holds for him, it is a future lived in the same relationship with the Spirit, who leads him on in the process of making him a mature Christian. In this process as a Christian he will recognize the need for the Holy Spirit to have a larger place in his life. He will also be inspired to express more completely his love for Christ by making a deeper commitment of himself to God through a full consecration of himself to Him. As a child of God, he at times may be conscious of a lack in his spiritual life and an awareness of impurities in his heart which are not compatible with his desire to be a total Christian. There may be some clashes between self-will and the will of God for him. He may find that while he walks in the Spirit there may be in him an occasional conflict between the flesh and the Spirit. Realizing this condition, he acknowledges his need to be filled or baptized with the Spirit, to be cleansed from these impurities, and to have his life brought into an inner unity with Christ as its center. He prays, he confesses his need, he places his total self upon God's altar as a dedicated gift to Him. At the same time he appropriates the provisions which Christ made to meet his present need, and by faith in Christ is baptized or filled with the Holy Spirit. His heart is purified by faith.

In this deepening of his relationship he is released to fully belong to Christ in a life of obedience and trust and service. This fullness of the Spirit, this being sanctified wholly, is a gracious experience for him. But it is not an appendage; rather it is an integral part of his person. It is the beginning of a new period in life more satisfying to him and more glorifying to God.

This process of salvation may be likened to the steps a person pursues in his education. First the child graduates from the grade school. Later comes his graduation from high school, and still later his participation in commencement exercises of a college or university. Perhaps he will be a participant in future ceremonies if he pursues graduate studies. But however far he goes in the process of education, it is the one person who is going through each of these important steps. His life is not divided into separate, unrelated areas, such as his first experience in education in grade school, his second experience in high school, and his third experience in college. These educational stages are but a part of the total process of his becoming an educated person.

The word *salvation* is inclusive of all the workings of God with man in spiritual life. It includes the gracious experiences of justification, regeneration, sanctification, and glorification. While there are different crisis experiences, each is a part of the one process of salvation. They are steps in his deepening relationship with God in the development of his life as a child of God. These different experiences are merged into one life which is in the process of becoming a mature Christian. The advantage of this process in salvation over the educational process is the continuing presence of the same Teacher. This is the person of the Holy Spirit, who motivates him and helps him to correlate all these spiritual experiences into an effective Christian life.

Chapter
THREE

A New Life-style

Through the work of the Holy Spirit in entire sanctification Christians *"are brought into a state of entire devotement to God."* This is the statement of our creed.

What is meant by devotement? Devotement belongs to the word family of *devote,* which suggests the total giving of oneself in all seriousness and earnestness to God for Him to have and use as He desires. The words *devote, dedicate,* and *consecrate* are synonymous. A state of devotement to God means, therefore, the living of a life which is fully devoted, dedicated, or consecrated to God. *Devotion,* which belongs to this same word family, involves loyalty, faithfulness, and deep affection. So the word *devotement* is all bound up with love. This is the inspiration for such living—love for God, which is brought about by the love of God being shed abroad in a person's heart by the Holy Spirit (Rom. 5:5).

This scripture is important if we are to understand what it means to be fully devoted to God. Is this love shed abroad in the heart a one-time gift, a once-for-all act of the Holy Spirit? Or is it a continued flooding of the heart with the love of God because of the continuing presence of the Holy Spirit in the life? Many translators and commentators, of which Dr. James Moffatt is one, indicate that it is a continuing act. His translation is: "God's love floods our hearts through the holy Spirit which has been given to us." Dr. C. H. Dodd makes this comment:

> The meaning of this very fundamental statement is not simply that we have become aware that God loves us, but that in the same experience in which we receive a deep and undeniable assurance of His love for us, that love becomes the central motive of our moral being. Since the nature of God Himself is love, in giving us love He imparts to us something of His own nature.[1]

Dr. Meyer is quoted as saying, "The divine love [is] effectually present in the heart through the Holy Spirit." Another writer says, "The souls of believers are flooded with God's love, which is in fact the presence of the Paraclete."[2] Dr. Adam Clarke says, "This love is the spring of all our actions; it is the motive of our obedience; the principle through which we love God. . . . By the Holy Spirit's energy it [love] is diffused and pervades every part."[3]

These statements indicate that the love of God shed abroad in our hearts is effectively present in our lives continually through the presence of the Holy Spirit. This makes possible a state of devotement to God.

Indeed this life-style is a present and continuing activity. It gets us away from "the experience we received years ago," when through the baptism with the Holy Spirit we were entirely sanctified, to a continuing life of love in the Spirit. This makes it a growing relationship. True, it was a great moment in our lives when we were filled with the Spirit. It was a life-changing moment of which we have many precious memories. But the work of the Spirit in sanctification was the door through which we came into the "state of devotement to God," or the life of holiness. In developing this state of life—this growth in grace—we keep moving more and more away from the entrance door of experience into a greater knowledge of God. We find a deeper life in the Holy Spirit and a fuller enjoyment of His presence and power in our lives. We enjoy a more effective life of trust and obedience in active service for Him.

In this development we experience more and more of the provisions of Christ for His children, become more aware of the riches of His grace, and have a better understanding of God's purposes for us. These advances in the spiritual life take us farther and farther away from the door through which we came into this expanding life we now enjoy in His presence and fellowship. The reality of the presence of God gives us cause for greater rejoicing, for indeed He is "God in the present tense," bringing to us all the benefits and blessings that this implies. We have a new life-style; we are living in a state of devotement to God, in a precious relationship with Him.

A Challenge to Reach the Best

To live a life of devotement to God, a sanctified life, means that we desire more and more to be what Christ, our loving Lord, wants us to be. *The Twentieth Century New Testament* gives this goal as being "destined . . . to be transformed into the likeness of his Son" (Rom. 8:29). This is God's purpose for us; this is our destiny. We must accept it and make it our own purpose. We must work with God in full determination of heart to fulfill it.

There are so many good things Christians can be involved in that it is easy for this activity to keep them from obtaining God's best for them spiritually. One must learn to choose what is the most meaningful and enriching. Perhaps Paul had something like this in mind when he prayed for the Philippian Christians: "I pray that your love will keep on growing more and more, together with true knowledge and perfect judgement, so that you will be able to choose what is best" (Phil. 1:9-10, TEV). This calls to mind the familiar bit of verse:

> *Good, better, best,*
> *And may we never rest*
> *Until our good is better*
> *And our better best.*

Paul's prayer was that God's people may have the knowledge and judgment to "choose what is best" from among the many good things that surround them. This choosing the best is a very essential discipline in the life of devotement to God. We can do no better in this discipline than to follow the example of Paul when he said: "We therefore make it our ambition, wherever we are, here or there, to be acceptable to him [the Lord]" (2 Cor. 5:9, NEB). He often spoke in terms of concentration. To the Philippians he wrote: "I do concentrate on this: I leave the past behind and with hands outstretched to whatever lies ahead I go straight for the goal—my reward the honor of my high calling by God in Christ Jesus" (Phil. 3:13-14, Phillips). We choose the best when we follow Paul's example: to make it our ambition, to concentrate on this, to have it as our aspiration to be transformed into the image of God's Son through our cooperation with the Holy Spirit.

Jesus stressed this thought of choosing the best by saying: "Seek ye first the kingdom of God, and his righteousness; and all these things shall be added unto you" (Matt. 6:33).

Some well-to-do Christian businessmen were driving across the nation to attend a convention. On the way they were discussing these words of Jesus. One confessed, "I am not seeking *first* the kingdom of God. I do seek His kingdom, but not *first*." Others admitted that they also were failing to put God first. Together they prayed, thanking God for His reproof, asking His forgiveness. Each dedicated himself anew to seek first, above and beyond everything else, Christ and His kingdom. They were transformed. God's Spirit fell upon them in abundance. Before reaching the convention city they won to Christ an attendant of a gasoline service station. At the convention the testimony they gave of the experience on the trip captured the hearts of many of those attending. Out of that convention, groups of Christian businessmen, now rededicated to seeking *first* the kingdom of God, went to different parts of the nation winning people to Christ.

We make progress toward the fulfillment of God's purpose for us when we seriously and sincerely give ourselves to seeking the best in the life of the Spirit.

THE CHRISTIAN FELLOWSHIP

The development of the life of devotement to God is found largely within the Christian fellowship. It is nurtured in relation to the people of God, the Church. Just as there is no substitute for the work of the Holy Spirit in the spiritual experiences of the new birth and entire sanctification, so there is no substitute for the work of the Holy Spirit within the Church for the development of Christian life.

God's great emphasis through Paul is upon the Church as the body of Christ. The Holy Spirit baptizes or incorporates believers into that body:

As the human body, which has many parts, is a unity, and those parts, despite their multiplicity, constitute one single body, so it is with Christ. For we were all baptized by the Spirit into

> *one body ... and we have all had experience of the same Spirit* (1 Cor. 12:12-13, Phillips).

Within this spiritual body the Holy Spirit works, uniting each member to the others. We share the life in Christ with other believers, and use our talents and special gifts of the Spirit for the good of each and all members of the body. This spiritual fellowship is also likened to a building:

> *So then you are no longer strangers and sojourners, but you are fellow citizens with the saints and members of the household of God, built upon the foundation of the apostles and prophets, Christ Jesus himself being the cornerstone, in whom the whole structure is joined together and grows into a holy temple in the Lord; in whom you also are built into it for a dwelling of God in the Spirit* (Eph. 2:19-22, RSV).

How precious and essential for our growth in grace is this unity of the body of Christ!

A picture of this wonderful sharing and unity is presented in the description of the Church following the Day of Pentecost:

> *And they devoted themselves to the apostles' teaching and fellowship, to the breaking of bread and the prayers. ... And all who believed ... sold their possessions and goods and distributed them to all, as any had need. And day by day, attending the temple together and breaking bread in their homes, they partook of food with glad and generous hearts, praising God and having favor with all the people. And the Lord added to their number day by day those who were being saved* (Acts 2:42-47, RSV).

This description of the Church is given in the setting of that day, but the essential elements of the fellowship of the body of Christ are presented as an example for us today.

There are many exhortations given to encourage and guide the people of God in this "fellowship of the Spirit" (Phil. 2:1), all of which call for the participation of each and all members of the body of Christ, as Paul said:

As God's prisoner, then, I beg you to live lives worthy of your high calling. Accept life with humility and patience, making allowances for one another because you love one another. Make it your aim to be at one in the Spirit, and you will inevitably be at peace with one another (Eph. 4:1-4, Phillips).

Perhaps the best summary of such exhortations is found in the twelfth chapter of Romans. After Paul says: "For as in one body we have many members, and all the members do not have the same function, so we, though many, are one body in Christ, and individually members one of another" (vv. 4-5, RSV), he gives many practical exhortations for life within the body (vv. 9-21). Changing these exhortations into affirmations, they could be stated as follows:

- I will love in all sincerity (v. 9).

- I will hate what is evil, holding fast to what is good (v. 9).

- I will have such love for the brotherhood as will breed a warmth of mutual affection (v. 10).

- I will outdo others in showing honor, or in showing a willingness to let the other man have the credit (v. 10).

- I will not allow slackness to spoil my work, but will

keep the fires of the Spirit burning as I do my work for the Lord (v. 11).

• I will rejoice in hope, basing my happiness on my hope in Christ. I will let hope keep me joyful (v. 12).

• When trials come to me, I will endure them patiently: or, I will stand firm when trouble comes (v. 12).

• I will steadfastly maintain the habit of prayer (v. 12).

• I will contribute to the needs of God's people and practice hospitality (v. 13).

• I will call down blessings on those who try to make my life a misery (v. 14).

• I will share the happiness of those who are happy, and the sorrow of those who are sad (v. 15).

• I will live in harmony with others; instead of being ambitious, I will associate with the humble folk (v. 16).

• I will not become set in my opinions, nor keep thinking how wise I am (v. 16).

• I will never pay back evil for evil, but will let my aims be such as all men count honorable (v. 17).

• I will, if possible and as far as it depends upon me, live peaceably with all (v. 18).

• I will not take vengeance into my own hands, but will stand back and let God punish if He chooses to (v. 19).

• I will obey God's word which says, "If your enemy is hungry, feed him; if he is thirsty, give him a drink; by doing this you will heap live coals on his head" (v. 20, NEB).

• I will not let evil conquer me, but will use good to defeat evil (v. 21).

(The writer is indebted to several of the late translations of the New Testament for some thoughts and words used in these affirmations.)

CHILDREN OF HOPE

Hope fills a large place in the life of one who is entirely devoted to God. The "not yet" is always intruding into the "here and now," moving us forward toward the new, the coming things and bringing us inspiration, courage, and faith.

When Peter exhorted his readers to holiness of life he said:

> *Wherefore gird up the loins of your mind, be sober, and hope to the end for the grace that is to be brought unto you at the revelation of Jesus Christ; as obedient children, not fashioning yourselves according to the former lusts in your ignorance: but as he which hath called you is holy, so be ye holy in all manner of conversation* (1 Pet. 1:13-15).

Hope is given here as the inspiration for the life of holiness.

For Paul, hope was a source of courage in his persecutions:

> *I consider that the sufferings of this present time are not worth comparing with the glory that is to be revealed to us. For the creation waits with eager longing for the revealing of the sons of God; . . . and not only the creation, but we ourselves, who have the first fruits of the Spirit, groan inwardly as we wait for adoption as sons, the redemption of our bodies. For in this hope we are saved* (Rom. 8:18-19, 23-24, RSV).

He reveals the inspiration brought by hope in another statement:

> *For this slight momentary affliction is preparing for us an eternal weight of glory beyond all comparison, because we look not to the things that are seen but to the things that are unseen; for the things that are seen are transient, but the things that are unseen are eternal* (2 Cor. 4:17-18, RSV).

The relation of hope to the life of holiness is stressed by Peter:

> *In view of the fact that all these things are to be dissolved, what sort of people ought you to be? Surely men of good and holy character, who live expecting and earnestly longing for the coming of the day of God. True, this day will mean that the heavens will disappear in fire and the elements disintegrate in fearful heat, but our hopes are not set on these but on the new heavens and the new earth which he has promised us, and in which nothing but good shall live. Because, my dear friends, you have a hope like this before you, I urge you to make certain that such a day would find you at peace with God and man, clean and blameless in his sight* (2 Pet. 3:11-14, Phillips).

Another scripture which emphasizes the value of hope is,

> *For the grace of God has appeared for the salvation of all men, training us to renounce irreligion and worldly passions, and live sober, upright, and godly lives in this world, awaiting our blessed hope, the appearing of the glory of our great God and Saviour Jesus Christ, who gave himself for us to redeem us from all iniquity and*

> *to purify for himself a people of his own who are zealous of good deeds* (Titus 2:11-14, RSV).

The mystery of the future ("looking for that blessed hope") ever moves us onward in anticipation. This is ever the inspiration to us for a life of holiness. Another word from John along this line could be added here:

> *Here and now we <u>are</u> God's children. We don't know what we shall become in the future. We only know that, if reality were to break through, we should reflect his likeness, for we should see him as he really is! Every one who has at heart a hope like that keeps himself pure* (1 John 3:2-3, Phillips).

The kingdom of God into which we have been born by the Spirit (John 3:5) is a present reality of righteousness, and peace, and joy in the Holy Spirit (Rom. 14:17), but it is also a hope which moves us toward its final fulfillment in God's eternal reign. Along the way, God continues to inspire us by His presence as He makes all things new. The future triumph is always before us.

People tend to accept the present with little or no expectation of any change. They are satisfied with the status quo. Even some who profess to be entirely sanctified don't expect much change in their lives beyond the initial experience. Their lives are clean, they harm no one, they give support to the church with their tithes and offerings and attendance, but they seek no expanding spiritual life. They do little in the way of becoming effective Christians. Their hope is limited to the expectations of finally reaching heaven by the grace of God.

But God wants to give us a new horizon. We are predestined to become conformed to the image of His Son. He sets before us a hope in which we will more and more be transformed into that image. He wants us to lift up our eyes to see what we may become, to catch a vision of our full possibilities. This hope of future fulfillment reaches back into the present life, inspiring us now to give ourselves more and more to a growing fellowship with Christ and an increasing enjoyment in the fellowship of the Church. Here is the motivation we need to fulfill the disciplines necessary for making progress toward that goal. This is the essence of hope which is desiring with the expectation of fulfillment. Christ is always going before us and in the end "we shall be like him; for we shall see him as he is." Such inspiration of hope prompted Paul to write, "I press on, hoping to take hold of that for which Christ once took hold of me" (Phil. 3:12, NEB).

The Church—the body of Christ—is here in the world to do what He would do if He were here. Every promise He gives of future victory for the Church inspires us as we work with and for Him in our world. The Church is not the creature of a passing moment; it is God's medium for proclaiming the gospel of Christ to the entire world. This affirmation of Jesus, "And I, if I be lifted up from the earth, will draw all men unto me" (John 12:32), presents a hope to the Church as well as an obligation to lift Him up as the Saviour of the world. If He is thus shown, people will be drawn to Him.

God is with us now in His promises as well as in His presence. That is why "the future is as bright as the promises of God," and that is why we work toward the fulfilling of His mission for the Church. We do so in the same strength of the Spirit and devotement to God as we do in our individual lives, as we seek to become conformed to the image of God's Son.

WE LIVE IN THE WORLD

Where must a sanctified Christian live this life of "devotement to God"? Right here "in this present world."

The world changes so rapidly (and most of the time not to our liking) that occasionally there is a desire within to "get away from it all." Some of us would agree with the title of a popular play, *Stop the World; I Want to Get Off.* But there is no "getting off." This is our world, the only one we can live in, however we may feel about it. The truth is, if the world ever needed the presence and influence and service of people who are living in a state of devotement to God, it needs it now.

Jesus had us in mind when He prayed, "I pray not that thou shouldest take them out of the world, but that thou shouldest keep them from the evil" (John 17:15). How then are we to live in this world? Not as complainers, sourpusses, and condemners (cf. John 3:17), but as those who enjoy all the good of the world; for, after all, our earth is full of the glory of God (Isa. 6:3). Furthermore, we are to be witnesses by life and in word to the hope that we know, and to make known to people everywhere the gospel of Christ, which is the power of God to salvation to all who believe.

Is not Jesus saying in His prayer that the world always needs His people—people who are fully devoted to Him? He said of us, "Ye are the salt of the earth"—people who give flavor and meaning to life and who are as an antiseptic and preservative in it to keep mankind from total destruction. He also said, "Ye are the light of the world"—guiding lights to a world which has lost its way, which lives in darkness and confusion, and which needs a light to guide it toward life and light and salvation in Christ.

At the same time, God's people need the world even with all its evils. It is through their experiences in the world that they develop as Christians and are made strong in character. There is no better place in God's universe for developing saints than right here in our world. There is no other place in which Christians can give such saving help and service. In this relationship they may "look on the world through the eyes of Christ," and bring to it a hopeful message in His name.

Jesus stresses something else, something which dispels all fears we may have because of the evils in our world: "I pray . . . that thou shouldest keep them from the evil" (John 17:15). This includes both the evils of our world and the evil one. The emphasis must be placed on the words *thou* and *keep*. We are surrounded by evils, but we are also living in a relationship with God. We are the objects of His loving care; we are in His keeping. We are like the people Paul addressed: "To all the saints *in* Christ Jesus which are *at* Philippi" (Phil. 1:1, emphasis mine). We live *in* Christ at an address *in* this world.

So as we live in "a state of devotement to God" we are not living in anxiety because of the evils of the world around us. Rather we are living in the consciousness that we are in the keeping of One "who is able to keep . . . [us] from falling, and to present . . . [us] faultless before the presence of his glory with exceeding joy" (Jude 24).

Because of our relationship to Him we are, as Jesus said, "no more sons of the world than I am" (John 17:16, Phillips). The world is devoted to things and ways of living which are the very opposite to those to which we have given our allegiance. We do not share its loves, its attitudes, its ideals, its godless way of living, its evils. But while the earth is our home we must give to it all we can to make it a better place in which to live. As we associate with the people in our world, we have the privilege of witnessing to them of the saving grace of God through the power of the Holy Spirit. We, like Paul, have a debt to pay to our world. We are under obligation to do our best to bring Christ's saving message to all people.

Another factor related to God's people being kept from

evil and being useful in the world is mentioned by Jesus: "Sanctify them through thy truth, thy word is truth" (v. 17). What did Jesus mean by "sanctify them"? A partial answer is found further on in the prayer, "For their sakes I sanctify myself, that they also might be sanctified through the truth" (v. 19). Jesus needed no cleansing from sin, so His sanctifying himself meant something other than cleansing. It meant His complete dedication or devotement to the Father's will, especially as He met "the hour [which] is come" (v. 1)—the hour of His decision and agony in the Garden of Gethsemane and of His crucifixion. Here He came face-to-face with the special will of the Father, so He sanctified or devoted himself to the doing of that special will. "Abba, Father," He prayed, "all things are possible unto thee; take away this cup from me: nevertheless not what I will, but what thou wilt" (Mark 14:36). Here is a wonderful example of what it means to live in "a state of entire devotement to God"—"Thy will, not mine, be done."

This is part of what it means for us to be sanctified; for, because of our moral impurities and sin, sanctification for us means the cleansing of our hearts. It involves removal of anything which would keep us from that state of devotement to God. It includes also the full consecration or dedication of ourselves to God that His purposes and His will may be done in and through our lives. Our being sanctified is made possible through what Jesus did in His sanctifying himself "for their sakes."

In the prayer of Jesus He not only asked for His people to remain *in* the world, although they were not *of* the world; He also said that in His mission for them they were to be *for* the world. "As thou hast sent me into the world, even so have I also sent them into the world" (v. 18). In other words, Jesus is looking for the Church, the body of

Christ in the world, to continue to fulfill His mission to the world.

What was Jesus sent into the world to do? "God sent not his Son into the world to condemn the world; but that the world through him might be saved" (John 3:17). He sends His cleansed and Spirit-filled people into the world on the same mission on which He himself was sent—that the world might be saved.

His mission in the world is also stated in the prophetic words of Isaiah as read by Jesus in the synagogue of Nazareth:

> *The Spirit of the Lord is upon me, because he hath anointed me to preach the gospel to the poor; He hath sent me to heal the brokenhearted, to preach deliverance to the captives, and recovering of sight to the blind, to set at liberty them who are bruised, to proclaim the acceptable year of the Lord* (Luke 4:18-19).

In this statement of Jesus' mission, people from every area of human need are included. As Jesus read it, the statement had social and political meaning to the hearers as well as deep spiritual significance. If this is the mission of Jesus to the world, He has sent us on that same mission. As we through the Spirit fulfill this mission to the best of our ability, we are bringing redemptive and creative changes into the lives of individuals and into society as a whole. We learn more about how to fulfill our mission to our world as we see how Jesus went about doing good, and healing all that were oppressed.

All classes of people were blessed by Jesus' ministry. He was especially open to the outcasts. The beggars, no doubt as dirty and unattractive as are oriental beggars today, received His gracious help. The lepers, afflicted with the most loathsome of all diseases, felt His touch and heard His word of cleansing. The blind, the deaf, the dumb, the demon-possessed were the recipients of His loving concern and healing power. These are the people who were ordinarily passed by and shunned, but Jesus served them. None were so evil that He passed them by; none were beyond His love and concern. He delivered Mary Magdalene from seven devils; He treated the woman guilty of adultery as a person worthy of His salvation, and He changed her life. The same was true of the street-woman (Luke 7:36-50), and of the woman of Sychar in Samaria (John 4:6-30). He saved, He healed, He blessed people without their asking anything of Him. He cleansed lepers who forgot to return to say, "Thank You." He brought salvation into the house of a despised tax gatherer in Jericho named Zacchaeus. He had an open heart to all who came to Him. He cared about the physical needs of people. He was concerned for His own disciples when they were in danger and distress, and by His power stopped the winds and calmed the sea. He was most patient with people who were slow to learn and those of little faith. What an example! He "went about doing good" epitomizes His life. He sends us, you and me, into our world on this same mission; He would have us go about *doing* good.

He cares how we respond to people and to their needs —whether or not we do what we can to help them. A person living "in a state of devotement to God" will be challenged by the opportunities for helping the people Jesus mentions in this statement:

> *"'I was hungry and you gave me food, I was thirsty and you gave me drink, I was a stranger and you welcomed me, I was naked and you clothed me, I was sick and you visited me, I was in prison and you came to me.'* . . . *'Lord, when did we see thee hungry and feed thee, or thirsty*

and give thee drink?' . . . 'Truly, I say to you, as you did it to one of the least of these my brethren, you did it to me'" (Matt. 25:35-40, RSV).

Within the mission Jesus has assigned us is His great commission, "Go ye into all the world, and preach the gospel to every creature" (Mark 16:15). Every person throughout the world deserves to hear the gospel of Christ. It will do us well to remember that the world begins right under our feet, not out at our nation's borders. We are challenged to give the gospel to our home community, then to reach out to people within our reach, as well as to those in the far reaches of the earth.

Let us look at the great promise Jesus made to His followers concerning the coming of the Holy Spirit and His working through them: "And when he is come [to you], he will reprove the world of sin, and of righteousness, and of judgment" (John 16:8). This translation may help us: "And when he comes he will prove to the people of the world that they are wrong about sin, and about what is right, and about God's judgment" (TEV).

This states Christ's mission and our mission clearly. This promise should lift our vision to see the need and inspire us to do all we can through the presence and power of the Holy Spirit working in and through us. May we be effective channels which God can use to bring the people of our world to know what Christ can do in their lives.

Let us look also at the last recorded words of Jesus spoken just before His ascension: "'But you shall receive power when the Holy Spirit has come upon you; and you shall be my witnesses in Jerusalem and in all Judea and Samaria and to the end of the earth'" (Acts 1:8, RSV). Here is found both the mission and the equipment needed by all persons who would follow the Master completely.

What a privilege! What an opportunity there is for responsible Christians, people devoted to Christ, in our world today! We can help fulfill the mission for which Jesus came into this world and which He has given to us.

* * *

We have before us an ideal, the purpose of God for us, namely, to become conformed to the image of His Son. This is done through a developing process, a growing relationship, a "being changed into his likeness from one degree of glory to another . . . [by] the Lord who is the Spirit" (2 Cor. 3:18, RSV). We do not become conformed to His image merely in one or two steps. Although this conformity begins with the crisis experiences in the work of the Spirit in regeneration and entire sanctification, it continues moment by moment as we walk in the Spirit and through His help keep pressing on toward the goal. This process of development requires patience and determination. It calls upon us to conquer, by God's help, any spirit of discouragement or any temptation to be self-satisfied or to be content with present achievements.

Always we need to remember that in these periods of test we have in us the presence of the One who, in every respect, has been tempted as we are (Heb. 4:15). We do well also to keep in mind the kind of Father we have: "Like as a father pitieth his children, so the Lord pitieth them that fear him. For he knoweth our frame; he remembereth that we are dust" (Ps. 103:13-14). We are reminded of the patience of Jesus in His working with His disciples to make them what He had called them to become. Especially is Peter a good example. How patient Jesus was with him as He worked to make him the rock He said he would become! We can be sure He will be as patient with us in our weaknesses, our failures, our stumbling efforts. Is He not as interested in our becoming substantial Christians as He was in making Peter the rock? In this developing relationship with Him we can learn from the musician who day by day, in success or in failure, keeps pursuing the goal of becoming an accomplished performer. Especially should this be true when we know our goal is to be conformed to the image of Jesus Christ himself, and to fulfill His mission to our world. What better motto can we have than: "Let us not grow weary in well-doing, for in due season we shall reap, if we do not lose heart" (Gal. 6:9, RSV).

Chapter
FOUR

Life in Relation

The life of holiness is one of relationship with Christ in obedience and love. This stresses another phase of our creedal statement on entire sanctification, that through this experience believers are brought into "the holy obedience of love made perfect." Love is then the motivating factor for our being responsible Christians in our relationship with Christ, with other Christians, and with people of our world.

The Meaning of Love

There are four Greek words used in the Bible for which in our English language we have only one word, *love*. Therefore in translating from the original into English all four words must be compressed into our word *love*. The Greek has the word *storge*, which relates primarily to love within the family; *eros*, which is most often used for love between the sexes; *philia*, which is used generally for warm and close friendship; and *agape*, which is self-giving love, a manifestation of goodwill—more descriptive of a quality of person than of a *kind* of love. *Agape* is used in its different forms about 250 times in the New Testament.

The first three words have an emotional background, meaning something that happens to us, like falling in love, etc. But *agape* (love) is different. We do not "fall into" *agape* (love); to love, in the *agape* sense, is to love purposefully with an "unconquerable benevolence and invincible goodwill" which is not governed by the emotions. This is why we can be commanded, "Thou shalt love [*agape*] the Lord thy God. . . . Thou shalt love [*agape*] thy neighbour as thyself." And this love includes the total person: "with all thy heart, and with all thy soul, and with all thy mind, and with all thy strength" (Mark 12:30-31).

Agape is God's unchangeable love for man. That is why nothing can separate us from His love. His love is without limitations and it embraces all the people of the world. In *agape*, Jesus came as man into the world and lived, loved, and served people with His total self, and in the end "gave himself a ransom for all" (1 Tim. 2:6).

It is *agape* which we have for God, for all mankind, and for each other within the Christian fellowship. It is the motivation for all true Christian service—a service which embraces people of all kinds, races, creeds, nations, social standings, and moral conditions. It encompasses all types of human dispositions. It is love which always seeks to do good and bring blessing to others. While *agape* involves a deliberate act of the will of man, Christian *agape* is possible only in persons who have the Holy Spirit dwelling in them, for it is "the fruit of the Spirit" (Gal. 5:22; Rom. 15:30; Col. 1:8). It is love born of a personal relationship with Christ. The best description of this kind of love is found in the thirteenth chapter of First Corinthians.

This is the love which, Jesus said, is demonstrated by God in making His sun to shine upon the evil and the good and sending rain on the just and the unjust. It is the love with which we are to love our enemies (which is a problem for many people). We should realize that Jesus does not ask us to love our enemies as we love our own family, nor to love them as we do our friends; we are to love our enemies in the spirit of *agape,* which says, "No matter what you have done to me, I will not seek revenge, nor will I harm you; rather, I will seek nothing but your highest good." This means taking a positive attitude toward the enemy, an attitude of helpfulness wherever and whenever we have the opportunity. Abraham Lincoln is quoted as saying, "I have lost many enemies by making them my friends." This is the spirit of *agape.*

Because *agape* requires a deliberate act of the will and of the total person, it may seem that it is something cold and mechanical. It is far from that. While *agape* does not primarily involve the emotions, it is not always without an emotional expression. It is the source of our most glorious and satisfying relationships. It is reflected in our relationship with God through Jesus Christ, our love for Him, our relationships in the Christian fellowship, and in our Christian service for people about us. It is the inspiration of "the holy obedience of love made perfect."

The word "perfect" has been bothersome to many people. But what do we mean by *perfect?* The dictionary defines *perfect* as "having all the qualities belonging to its nature." Since the word *perfect* is used here exclusively in relation to Christian love, *perfect love* means having all the qualities belonging to such love.

Jesus exhorted the people in His Sermon on the Mount, "Be ye therefore perfect, even as your Father which is in heaven is perfect" (Matt. 5:48). R. George Smith says this means

> to be wholly turned, with the whole will and being, to God, as He is turned to us. This is a response of obedience and of effort carried out in faith. It is the call to

purify our hearts and to will one thing. This command falls within a religious situation, not simply a moral situation of improving our conduct by ever more strenuous efforts or the like. . . . Perfect is something related to God and coming to us by our contact with God . . . as a gift. . . . Our relation to Him determines our share in this kind of wholeness.[1]

The Scriptures teach that this perfection of love is not of human origin; it comes through our relationship with God. It is the love of God shed abroad in our hearts by the Holy Spirit who is given unto us (Rom. 5:5). It is related to our dwelling in God and God dwelling in us (1 John 4:16); to our obeying the words of Jesus (1 John 2:5; John 14:23), and to our loving one another (1 John 4:12). It is God's love which is perfected in us, and our love which is made perfect (1 John 4:12, 17).

Love reaches its peak [is made perfect] in that we are certain that on the day of judgment we have nothing to fear, because our relationship to this world is the same as his [Jesus'] was. . . . Perfect love banishes fear (1 John 4:17-18, Barclay).

The Obedience of Love

This "obedience of love made perfect" is the fruit of the Sanctifier, the Holy Spirit. He is God in the present tense dwelling in our hearts and lives. Peter speaks of it twice. He addresses the Epistle to the "elect according to the foreknowledge of God the Father, through sanctification of the Spirit, unto obedience and sprinkling of the blood of Jesus." And, "Seeing ye have purified your souls in obeying the truth through the Spirit unto unfeigned love of the brethren, see that ye love one another with a pure heart fervently" (1 Pet. 1:2, 22).

Obedience, as we are thinking of it here, is more than

the accumulation of numerous acts of obeying. It means, rather, a mode or condition of life, a consistent attitude of obedience which says, I have no other thought than to be obedient. The obedience of love goes a little farther, and says, I love to obey God; or as the Psalmist said, "I delight to do thy will, O my God" (Ps. 40:8). This obedience is motivated by our love to Christ and is encouraged and made possible through the presence of the Holy Spirit in our lives.

Jesus is our wonderful Example of obedience. The attitude of His entire life is expressed in His own words: "'It is meat and drink for me to do the will of him who sent me until I have finished his work'" (John 4:34, NEB), and, "I do always those things that please him [the Father]" (John 8:29). His coming death seemed to present a problem to Him. On one occasion He said, "'Now is my soul troubled. And what shall I say? "Father, save me from this hour"? No, for this purpose I have come to this hour. Father, glorify thy name'" (John 12:27-28, RSV). When He actually faced that hour in Gethsemane He seemed to question, Is there not some other way? For He prayed, "'Father, if thou art willing, remove this cup from me; nevertheless not my will, but thine, be done'" (Luke 22:42, RSV). One thing is evident in this experience: There was never a question about His obedience, for He said, "Nevertheless not as I will, but as thou wilt" (Matt. 26:39).

We have times when we do not understand our situations, when we have questions, when we shrink from what is required of us in obedience. But in all this God understands, and in the end our love for Him and our desire to obey Him enables us by His Spirit to say, "Thy will, not mine, be done." And when we have said that, the matter is settled. We find so much joy in doing the will of God and are so blessed by the fruits of obedience that we refrain from looking back and recalling with reservations "the great price we paid" to obey God.

Another wonderful example of this obedience in love is seen in the life of the Apostle Paul. He gave expression to the powerful motive which inspired his life and service when he said, "The love of Christ constraineth us" (2 Cor. 5:14). The love of Christ had mastered him until he served and suffered for Christ solely because his love for Christ constrained him to do it. There was no law, no reward, no honor, no remuneration, that could have been offered him that would make him do what he did. He lived, he loved, he served, he suffered, solely because of the compulsion within which stemmed from Christ's love. This is the secret of "the holy obedience of love made perfect." It is not the principle of obeying a law; it is loving and following a Person, Jesus Christ, our Saviour and Lord.

We serve Christ and His Church and the world best by doing those things we do because we love Christ and look for no other compensation. Perhaps we do well to ask ourselves: What am I doing in my life solely because I love Christ? What am I doing for Christ beyond what I myself could do if the Holy Spirit were not working in and through me? It is a tragic commentary on the low temperature of our love for Christ when Christians must be pressured, bribed by rewards in contests, or otherwise coaxed and threatened to get them to do things for Christ, for the Church, and for the world. They would be doing these things spontaneously if they were constrained by the love of Christ, or if they were giving Him "the holy obedience of love made perfect." When the love of Christ constrains us, we give ourselves freely to acts of service, helpful attitudes, inspiring words, and unselfish deeds. We even suffer for Him, not because we are compelled by law or seek some reward or credit, but solely because we love Christ and want to express that love in ways which are pleasing to

Him. This is the kind of loving and obeying that takes place when the Holy Spirit has come to us in His fullness and as we walk in this relationship with Him in our world.

RESPONSIBLE CHRISTIANS

A responsible Christian is one who is trustworthy, dependable, and reliable. He is one upon whom God can count to fulfill well the responsibilities of the Christian life. Mainly this is the result of his being filled with the Holy Spirit or sanctified wholly.

These responsibilities are not arbitrarily placed upon us by a supreme God; they are the responsibilities we accept, responsibilities we have chosen because we love Christ. Actually they are privileges found in a relationship of love to Christ. This way of responsible living is not a bondage; it is the free expression of a heart which truly loves Christ. These responsibilities are comparable to those of a happily married couple. They make sacrifices for each other; they express their love one for the other both by spoken words and actions; they have a concern which puts the other first in matters of mutual interest; and desire to do what they can, even to going the second mile, to develop a satisfying married life. The responsibilities may also be likened to those of a musician who is so devoted to developing his skill and technique to become an accomplished performer that he gladly and willingly imposes upon himself the restrictions and efforts required to reach his goal.

These responsibilities are not thought of as laws; they are privileges—ways for us to express our love for Christ. We do not wake up in the morning and say, "This is a new day; I *must* fulfill my responsibilities for living a sanctified life today." No. We say, "Lord, I love You. Your love is so blessed and wonderful to me that today by the help of Your

Spirit I want to live responsibly in whatever Your love will bring to me. I want to express Your love in my love and concern for other people in bringing blessing to them and in some way turning their minds toward You."

Paul stated these responsibilities of entire devotement to God as he experienced them in terms of being a debtor. "I feel myself under a sort of universal obligation," he said; "I owe something to all men, from cultured Greek to ignorant savage. That is why I want as far as my ability will carry me, to preach the gospel to you who live in Rome" (Rom. 1:14-15, Phillips). He felt that the gospel had been given him as a trust, with all the responsibilities that were thus entailed. "Our message to you is true, our motives are pure, our conduct is absolutely aboveboard. We speak under the solemn sense of being entrusted by God with the gospel" (1 Thess. 2:4, Phillips).

He gives an insight into the master motive of his life in these words: "For the love of Christ controls us, because we are convinced that one died for all; therefore all have died. And he died for all, that those who live might live no longer for themselves but for him who for their sake died and was raised" (2 Cor. 5:14-15, RSV). In his efforts to improve relations between himself and the Corinthian church, he said: "I will most gladly spend and be spent for your good, even though it means that the more I love you, the less you love me" (2 Cor. 12:15, Phillips). Being a responsible Christian was no great burden to this great Christian, for his whole life was inspired by the love of Christ. That relationship turns any burden into a privilege.

Jesus stressed this responsibility of love in His third meeting with His disciples following His resurrection (John 21:14-22, RSV). In response to His question to Peter, "Do you love me more than these?" Peter said, "Yes, Lord; you know I love you." Three times Jesus asked Peter this question; three times Peter pledged his love, "Lord, you know that I love you," and three times Jesus attached responsibility to that pledge of love by Peter: "Feed my lambs," "Tend my sheep," "Feed my sheep" (vv. 15-18). Our love for Christ is demonstrated in the loving response we give to the obligations presented. In other words, Jesus was asking Peter to be a responsible Christian, and the story of his life from this time onward proves that indeed he was just that. Jesus' appeal to Peter, "Follow me" (vv. 19, 22), was also based on the love pledged by Peter. From then on no one followed Jesus more devotedly than did Peter.

Our being responsible Christians, or living in a state of devotement to God, demands of us personal development, or growth in grace, as Christians.

There are several statements of scripture which stress what God has destined us to be. For example: "He chose us in him before the foundation of the world, that we should be holy and blameless before him. He destined us in love to be his sons through Jesus Christ, according to the purpose of his will, to the praise of his glorious grace which he freely bestowed on us in the beloved" (Eph. 1:4-6, RSV). In Romans we read that we are "predestined to be conformed to the image of his Son" (8:29, RSV), or as Phillips translates it, "to bear the family likeness of his Son."

Who has predestined us in love to be His children? It is God, who also has predestined us to be conformed to the family likeness of His Son. Let us then open wide our hearts to the Holy Spirit, and may we be so deeply moved by our love for Christ as to work with Him in His efforts to make us into the likeness of himself. Let us realize too that the fulfillment of this destiny does not come through pleasant dreams, nor by easy living, nor by just saying words. This becoming conformed to the image of His Son is a developing process in which we as responsible Christians give ourselves fully and lovingly to the necessary disciplines required in the process. We know full well, of course, that only God can actually conform us to the family likeness of Christ, so we place our total dependence upon Him to bring the process to its desired end.

Paul gives a hint of how this process works in the lives of responsible Christians when he says, "But we all, with unveiled face beholding as in a mirror the glory of the Lord, are being transformed into the same image from glory to glory, just as from the Lord, the Spirit" (2 Cor. 3:18, NASB).

The challenging word for us in this process is "beholding"; that is, giving special attention to the glory of the Lord. This involves meditating upon Him and His glory, letting His image become imprinted upon our hearts, and following the Spirit as He leads us into an increasing relationship with Him and His glory. In this way He transforms us into the image of God's Son.

The attitude of responsible Christians in this process in relationship is to respond to God in ways like: "Yes, Lord; what would You have me to do?" "Which is the way, Lord?" "What insights have You to give me here?" "Would You have me to change my approach to this problem?" "Should I change the plan I have for working in this area?" "Would You have me change my attitude in this situation to one which is more loving?" "Should I make some adjustment in my personal relationships in order that I may manifest Your power and glory to others?" "What changes would You have me make within my own self?" etc. The right response to the Spirit in matters like these is the basis for our development toward being more and more conformed to the image of Jesus. This is how we deepen our devotement to God and grow in "the holy obedience of love made perfect."

Humility and Penitence

Life in relationship with God through the Holy Spirit is really the grace of God in action in human life. Grace is always something given when something else was deserved. It is the open heart and hand of God to us who merit nothing but His disfavor. It is positive, becoming an active principle in life: "Grace *reign[s]* through righteousness unto eternal life by Jesus Christ our Lord" (Rom. 5: 21, italics mine). It seems that here Paul uses *grace* almost as a synonym for the Holy Spirit, for both are given to undeserving persons.

Further, there is always the atoning presence of Christ with us, as well as His heavenly intercession for us. The early leaders of the holiness movement stressed strongly this fact by recognizing the need of our saying sincerely: "Every moment, Lord, I need the merits of Thy blood." John, the apostle, expresses it in these words: "If we walk in the light, as he is in the light, we have fellowship one with another, and the blood of Jesus Christ his Son cleanseth us [that is, continues to cleanse or keep us clean] from all sin" (1 John 1:7). The words "walk," "fellowship," continued "cleansing" involve relationship with God, who is the Light (v. 5); and with the Saviour, who keeps us clean as we fellowship with Him and His redeemed people. This is also the relationship we need to keep us clean in our dirty world and to make our witness effective to those who know not this fellowship.

Since we are always dependent upon God and others, the proper response for us is that of humility, particularly an attitude of unworthiness. Who am I that God should do so much for me and with me? Pride is the very opposite to walking with and having fellowship with God. Gratitude and thanksgiving as an abiding attitude of life is a true expression of humility.

We have many experiences in life which make us conscious of our creaturely weakness. For example, the fact that however "well saved" we are and however sincerely we endeavor to live out the relationship with Christ we enjoy, we are still human and at times we fall short of being all we want to be. Then we are weak when we should be strong. We may be overtaken in temptation and fail God. We fall short of what we should be in life's relationships, like not being the husband or wife we might be; not being the kind of parents we could be with a little more time and effort; not being the workmen we might be. We fail to give our best as Sunday school teachers or as members of the church board. We become casual in other church responsibilities. We pass by opportunities to witness for Christ and to do good to others. We neglect the essential devotional exercises which would make us stronger and more effective Christians, etc.

These are some of the attitudes or actions which grieve the Holy Spirit (Eph. 4:30). To grieve someone is to disappoint, to cause pain, to injure, to sadden that person. What husband and wife are there who have not grieved the other spouse? What did they do when this happened? Undertake divorce proceedings? No. The relationship was strained but not broken. So it is in our relationship with God. To grieve the Spirit is not to break relationship with Him. Certainly we are disappointed with ourselves and feel reproved as we recognize our failures and shortcomings. Our attitude under such circumstances must be one of sincere penitence. We must admit the offense without excuses, ask forgiveness, and on the basis of God's promise accept His gracious understanding and pardon. There must be a full reconciliation, with the strained condition entirely removed. With the married couple where one has grieved the other, these same steps are appropriate. It is a matter of "kissing and making up." All of which means that we must live in an attitude of penitence. Dr. H. Orton Wiley says:

> Penitence is that attitude which belongs to every mortal being recovered from sin, and as such will not only exist in every subsequent stage of life, but will have a place in heaven.... True repentance brings a change of mind, which followed by an act of saving faith, brings the soul into the state of initial salvation; and the continuance of penitence as a state makes possible the reception of further benefits and an abiding communion with God.[2]

If the wonderful relationship with God is to be maintained satisfactorily, we must keep an open mind and sensitive attitude toward Him. We must be ever ready to recognize and accept His warnings, His rebukes, His checks on our thinking and acting, and His leadership and guidance. He is in the process of bringing us to be conformed more and more to the image of His Son. And in this area of life, as in all others, through the Holy Spirit we remain responsible Christians, giving to Him "the obedience of love made perfect."

Chapter
FIVE

Called unto Holiness

God wants you to be like Him. Does that startle you? Well, look at what He says: "As he who called you is holy, be holy yourselves in all your conduct; since it is written, 'You shall be holy, for I am holy'" (1 Pet. 1:15-16, RSV). We should give special attention to this call, for it is stated six times in the Bible.

God is declared to be: "the high and lofty One that inhabiteth eternity, whose name is Holy . . . [who dwells] in the high and holy place, with him also that is of a contrite and humble spirit" (Isa. 57:15). This means that the One who inhabits eternity, "whose name is Holy," and who is in many aspects of His nature distant from us, is also God who is near to us. In fact He is so near that He dwells with persons right here on earth, persons who are of "a contrite and humble spirit." So as this Holy One who inhabits eternity calls us to become like Him, He is close enough to help us accept and fulfill that call. He is the Divine Person in relationship with man.

God is holy! What does that mean? To give any definition of the Infinite is beyond our ability, but that does not keep us from thinking about God and endeavoring to give some sort of explanation. Even theologians find it most difficult to give any clear meaning of *holy* as it is related to God. Generally they agree, however, that holiness is the sum total of all His moral attributes—His absolute purity; His freedom from all imperfections; the perfection of His wisdom, righteousness, faithfulness, justice, mercy, and love. But when we turn to the Scriptures we note that they speak not so much of the holiness of God as of "the Holy One." He is pictured as a Person to be known; a God to be reverenced, worshipped, and adored. For example, 27 times in the Book of Isaiah He is spoken of as "the Holy One of Israel."

There is a great difference between saying something about God and speaking of God himself. When we consider the holiness of God we set it out as a sort of separate entity —a thing. We can talk about it, examine it, and form conclusions concerning it. There is nothing sinful about that except when we substitute the thing for the Person. When we consider God, the Holy One, we are thinking about a Person who is with us. He is a God we can love and can know in personal relationship, and who in this relationship makes great changes in us and in our living. He is a God to be obeyed in love. But He always remains the high and lofty One who inhabits eternity, "whose name is Holy." We are always His creatures, unworthy of approaching His awesome presence; so we live in the realization that it is only through His love and grace that we can approach Him. Praise His name, He has opened the way for us to come to Him and live in a vital relationship with Him while we live in this world!

It was in this sense and with an awesome feeling that the prophet Isaiah saw Him (Isa. 6:1-7) as the thrice holy God, "high and lifted up." He heard the seraphim cry one to another, "Holy, holy, holy, is the Lord of hosts: the whole earth is full of his glory" (v. 3). But note the effect this vision had upon the prophet. As he saw the holy God, "high and lifted up," a reflection of that holiness penetrated his own self, revealing the impurities of his nature and of the people about him. So he cried, "Woe is me! for I am undone [I am speechless; I have no defense to bring]; because I am a man of unclean lips, and I dwell in the midst of a people of unclean lips: for mine eyes have seen the King, the Lord of hosts" (v. 5).

Here is a good example of what happens when a creature is confronted by the Creator, when the human meets the Divine. There is always humility and confession, a consciousness of total unworthiness to be in His presence. Here is also an example of what the Divine wants to do for the human, for God gave instruction for Isaiah's cleansing:

> *Then flew one of the seraphims unto me, having a live coal in his hand, which he had taken with tongs from off the altar: and he laid it upon my mouth, and said, Lo, this hath touched thy lips; and thine iniquity is taken away, and thy sin purged* (vv. 6-7).

God is the Holy One, the One who makes himself known to us as a Person. He is the One who cleanses the impure penitent and relates him in His love to himself in a glorious, strengthening fellowship.

God Calls Us to Holiness

As stated above, God is calling us to become like himself. "For God hath not called us unto uncleanness, but unto holiness. He therefore that despiseth, despiseth not man, but God, who hath also given unto us his holy Spirit" (1 Thess. 4:7-8). Two great truths are brought together in this statement: (1) God calls us unto holiness, and (2) He also gives His Holy Spirit to us.

If God should say, "I want you to be holy," then leave us to our own resources, we would be totally frustrated and defeated. God does call us to holiness, but He provides the means. He gives His Holy Spirit to us, so that He may make and keep us holy. This stresses the important truth that it is not through our own struggles and efforts that we become holy; it is solely through the work of the Holy Spirit, who is given to us. And it is through a living relationship with this Holy Spirit that we are kept clean in a dirty world.

Dr. Nels Ferré tells of a man, a carpenter, who in a conversation seriously said to him, "Dr. Ferré, won't you help us put the leaves back on the tree of life?" Dr. Ferré was startled by the question. He thought, We don't take leaves and put them back on living trees. Furthermore, according to the biblical account, the trouble was not with the tree of life, but with us who have become separated from it. What the man meant, said Dr. Ferré, was: "Help us find the purity, the relationship with God, the life of goodness and holiness, the life of meaning and purpose, the place where we can be back home with God, which was represented by the tree of life." It is to such a life that God calls us. He calls us to holiness.

God does not want His people to be the victims of their age. These Thessalonian Christians to whom Paul was writing were living in a most ungodly, immoral, and unclean age. It is difficult for us to conceive of the actual moral and spiritual condition which existed then, a condition which is vividly described in Rom. 1:18-32. But this call to holiness tells us that God is never on the side of uncleanness of any kind in any age. He calls us always away from these conditions which are contrary to His nature; He calls His people to holy living.

This call as it comes to us finds us living in an entirely different age or culture from theirs. But each culture has its dominant factors. Theirs was moral uncleanness; ours is a secular, technological society (though, of course, not without its moral decadence). It is secular in that people are self-sufficient. They give little or no place for God in their living as individuals, in their society, or in their industry and business. The result is that life is empty and without meaning. Our society is fast losing the ethical values which have been the foundation of our civilization. Within our culture are pockets of uncleanness not unlike those found in New Testament times. This is the result of our losing our moral and spiritual bearings.

Then too, we are becoming mastered by a technological monster of our own making. This monster is robbing us of our personal meaning and identity, making us about as much a part of the machine as are electronic products and computers. From these things we are receiving no true satisfaction. We are a lost generation, lost amid gadgets and machines of our own making which to a large degree have become our masters.

God's call to holiness comes to us in our culture as clearly as it came to the people of Paul's age. God has not called us to the emptiness and death of our secular/technological culture; He is calling us to holiness.

One of the most redeeming factors for us to note is that men long for the kind of life to which God is calling them. They want the leaves put back on the tree of life. Within every man there is a hunger for personal fulfillment, for love, healing, freedom, and righteousness. He seeks for a transcendent meaning of life which can be found only through the Holy Spirit bringing to and maintaining in him a life of holiness. A life like that is possible in this age when God is living in him. That is why God has given His Holy Spirit.

What we are thinking about is more than an ideal, more than theory or doctrine. We are thinking about man, about persons like us, you and me, who have the call to become intimately related to God through the presence of His Holy Spirit. He can bring into our lives the joy of living a life of holiness even in a contrary culture.

THE WILL OF GOD

Before we think more about this call to holiness, let us look at the preceding verses in this chapter. The word *for* ("for God hath not called us," etc.) relates Paul's thinking to what he has said in the verses before:

> *For ye know what commandments we gave you by the Lord Jesus. For this is the will of God, even your sanctification, that ye should abstain from fornication: that every one of you should know how to possess his vessel in sanctification and honour; not in the lust of concupiscence, even as the Gentiles which know not God: that no man go beyond and defraud his brother in any matter: because that the Lord is the avenger of all such, as we also have forewarned you and testified"* (1 Thess. 4:2-6).

This statement, "This is the will of God, even your sanctification," is the same as God saying, "I want you to be sanctified." But it is more. In the light of the further statement that He gives us His Holy Spirit, we may think of God saying, "I want you to be sanctified through My Spirit, whom I am giving you." This thought is further strengthened by Paul's later words, "And the very God of peace sanctify you wholly" (1 Thess. 5:23).

God does not take us out of the evil and immoral environment of our world, nor does He change our world for us. What He does do is to fortify us against the world's evils through a relationship with the Holy Spirit. He is truly God in the present tense, working in and through our lives. This gives us a reason for living in a world like ours. Through His purifying work and abiding presence we are not the victims of our age; rather, we are overcomers—"a living testimonial to the teaching of God our savior" (Titus 2:10, Phillips).

Paul lists also the results of our being sanctified through the Holy Spirit. Three are mentioned.

1. *Clean moral living.* "That [sanctification] entails first of all a clean cut with sexual immorality" (4:3, Phillips).

The words *that ye* bring us face-to-face with responsible Christian living. We must put forth an effort in cooperation with the Holy Spirit to live free from all uncleanness, not only from the outward acts of immorality, but from its inner desires (cf. Matt. 5:28).

These Thessalonian Christians were recent converts from among "the Gentiles which know not God" and who lived in the passion of lust (v. 5). They were now living for Christ, having made a clean cut with immorality. So this was an entirely new and different way of living for them, and it was made possible through the sanctifying power and presence of the Holy Spirit, whom God had given to them.

2. *Self-control.* "Every one of you should learn to control his body, keeping it pure and treating it with respect, and never regarding it as an instrument for self-gratification, as do pagans with no knowledge of God" (vv. 4-5, Phillips).

The King James Version reads, "That every one of you should know how to possess his vessel." Though some translators claim that *vessel* means *wife* in every place

Paul uses the word in relation to people it refers to the body. For example, in 2 Cor. 4:7, we read: "We have this treasure in earthen vessels," or as *The Amplified Bible* has it, "[frail, human] vessels of earth." Again, "If a man therefore purge [cleanse] himself from these, he shall be a vessel unto honour" (2 Tim. 2:21). God said of Saul (Paul) after his conversion, "He is a chosen vessel unto me" (Acts 9:15).

Of the body Paul said: "Your body is the temple of the Holy Ghost which is in you. . . . therefore glorify God in your body, and in your spirit, which are God's" (1 Cor. 6:19-20). He said of himself that he practiced personal discipline: "I keep under my body, and bring it into subjection"; or, "I am my body's sternest master" (1 Cor. 9:27, KJV, Phillips).

So Paul is saying that one result of being sanctified by the Holy Spirit is the ability one has "to possess his vessel [body] in sanctification and honour," not in lust, as do the people who do not know God. Every normal desire, appetite, and function of the body can find its fulfillment within these instructions: "keeping it pure and treating it with respect" (v. 4, Phillips).

3. *Respect for others.* "No one must try to overreach his fellowman in business, or try to exploit him, because, as we have already definitely told you, the Lord exacts the penalty for all such actions" (v. 6, Barclay).

The Holy Spirit, who in the work of sanctification helps each of us to have respect and appreciation for his own self and live in wholesome self-control, also helps us to regard and appreciate other persons in their individuality, their freedom, and their life-style. He enables us to be sensitive to them and their needs and to be sincere, honest, and aboveboard in all our relations with them in every area of life.

What the Call to Holiness Means

What does this call to holiness mean to us who live in a secular, technological age with all the tensions and pressures that it brings to us?

1. This call means *separateness*. It calls us to find a true center around which, by the help of the Spirit within us, we can organize satisfying and useful lives. As we thus glorify God in our lives, we are enabled to bring blessing to other people.

It is a fortunate time in any person's life when he discovers that he cannot do everything. He must decide on the right priorities for his life and devote himself definitely to them. Christians, particularly, must get down to the things that truly count and give themselves to them. They must separate themselves from things which are not consistent with their fulfilling God's call to holiness. Also this separated person has something to give to the people of our world, something he could not offer without this separation to God.

The primary meaning of holiness throughout the Bible is that of separateness. In the Old Testament particularly, *things* are said to be holy. For example, the Tabernacle, the place of worship for Israel in their wilderness journeys, along with its furnishings and vessels, was holy. Later, the Temple in Jerusalem was holy. People associated with worship ceremonies were holy. What made them holy? They were holy, not in the sense that they were possessed of moral quality, but because they had been separated from the common and ordinary use to be dedicated to God for use in His service and in worship. They were separated to God; hence they were holy. The thought of purity with respect to "holy" became more prominent in the New Testament, but separation is still the fundamental biblical meaning of the word.

This phase of holiness is stressed by Paul, when he

said: "Come out from among them, and be ye separate, saith the Lord, and touch not the unclean thing." This is a separation from evil. But holiness means more; it means separation or devotion to God and to that which is holy, for Paul continues: "And I will receive you, and will be a Father unto you, and ye shall be my sons and daughters, saith the Lord almighty" (2 Cor. 6:17-18). This separation was a means to a great end: "I will receive you." God is saying, "Separate yourselves from that, that indeed you may belong to Me." Is ever a greater privilege offered to us?

Holiness, then, means belonging to God, as Paul frequently stresses. The Christian has found in Christ the One who is worthy of his deepest devotion, of his sincerest appreciation, and of his most sacrificial service. His desire to love Him with all his heart is stronger than his love for anything else. This is the center around which, with the aid of the Holy Spirit, he will organize his life in this world. This is true consecration, for when Christ is the Center of our lives, we find this relationship to be most satisfying and it enables us to be fruitful in living the life of holiness.

Why does God have a separated or holy people in this world? Why does He have the Church? Jesus told His disciples what the Holy Spirit would do through His people in the world in these words: "And when he [the Holy Spirit] is come [to you], he will reprove the world of sin, and of righteousness, and of judgment" (John 16:8). It is through His separated people that the Holy Spirit reaches the world with the message of the gospel. It is the Holy Spirit within us who enables us to move on the conscience of the world to reprove the people "of sin, and of righteousness, and of judgment."

We need not say much in order to reprove. When we live in the Spirit, live our lives dynamically, live them in love, we then live in a way that brings blessing and good to others—in a way that reproves their sin but also turns their minds toward Christ. We follow the example of Jesus, who came into the world, not "to condemn the world; but that the world through him might be saved" (John 3:17).

To answer this call to holiness, to be entirely sanctified, and to live a life of holiness means, then, to be separated from all uncleanness, separated from the world's godless culture, and to be fully set apart to God. Yet we must live within this culture; it is our only world. Indeed it is our place for Christian service. It is the work of the Holy Spirit to "set apart" the people of God, both individually and collectively in the Church, so that the Spirit dwelling in them will work through them to turn others toward God.

2. The call to holiness is a call to *purity* in the center of life.

Purity is very difficult to define. About the simplest way to say it is: "Purity is what is left after impurities are removed." Purity is what is left after the Holy Spirit given to us has cleansed our hearts. Peter testified clearly to this when he explained to the church council what God did for the Gentiles in the home of Cornelius and for the disciples and others on the Day of Pentecost: "And God, which knoweth the hearts, bare them [the Gentiles] witness, giving them the Holy Ghost, even as he did unto us [at Pentecost]; and put no difference between us and them, purifying their hearts by faith" (Acts 15:8-9). So purity of heart is the work of God; it is not our own work. God purified their hearts by faith through the coming of the Holy Spirit upon them.

"But," someone asks, "what about the scriptures that ask us to purify ourselves?" For example,

> *Having therefore these promises, dearly beloved, let us cleanse ourselves from all filthiness*

of the flesh and spirit, perfecting holiness in the fear of God (2 Cor. 7:1).

Cleanse your hands, ye sinners; and purify your hearts, ye double-minded (Jas. 4:8).

And every man that hath this hope in him purifieth himself, even as he is pure (1 John 3:3).

These scriptures indicate that we have some responsibility for our cleansing. We are to do something preparatory to the cleansing done by the Holy Spirit. There are at least three things we must do to prepare, or cleanse ourselves, preliminary to God's great work of cleansing our hearts. They are:

a. We must acknowledge and renounce with all of our hearts all impurities. As the Holy Spirit reveals carnal dispositions and affections, pride, self-will, and other unholy factors in our lives, by His help we sincerely and honestly abhor and renounce them as we look to God earnestly and in faith to cleanse our hearts.

b. We must bring ourselves to the Source of all purity. We know that there is no way for us to truly cleanse ourselves from these impurities. God alone can fully cleanse us, so in deep contrition we come to Him with the cry upon our lips which was expressed by the Psalmist centuries ago, "Purge me . . . and I shall be clean: wash me, and I shall be whiter than snow" (Ps. 51:7). We come to Him, the Source of all cleansing, that indeed, through the blood of Jesus, He will cleanse us from all sin (1 John 1:7).

c. We make use of the means provided for our cleansing. We cleanse ourselves physically by making use of water and soap, applying them to the soiled areas and exerting the scrubbing action required. In other words, we cleanse ourselves by using the means provided for our physical cleansing. It is the same with heart cleansing. The means are described in the scriptures: "Seeing ye have purified your souls in obeying the truth through the Spirit" (1 Pet. 1:22); "If we walk in the light . . . the blood of Jesus Christ his Son cleanseth us from all sin" (1 John 1:7); and "purifying their hearts by faith" (Acts 15:9). The means provided for our cleansing is "obeying the truth through the Spirit," by "walking in the light," and "by faith." Thus we "cleanse ourselves" preparatory to the actual work of cleansing by God himself as we fully trust Him to now purify our hearts by faith.

There is strength in purity; there is a cohesion at the center of a life of holiness. This certainly means we live pure or clean lives, with pure motives, clean thinking, clean conversation, and high morals. It is a life of singleness of purpose to glorify God in our bodies and spirits, which are His (1 Cor. 6:20).

The philosopher Kierkegaard wrote a book stressing the theme "To be pure in heart is to will one thing." That is it. Jesus spoke of it as the "single" eye: "If . . . thine eye be single, thy whole body shall be full of light" (Matt. 6:22). Purity of heart means coming to the point where there is one dominant purpose in life. A full and meaningful relationship with the Holy Spirit brings us to the place where our supreme desire is to glorify God. This is living up to the creedal standard—"the state of devotement to God, and the holy obedience of love made perfect."

The emphasis is made in the New Testament on the new covenant in contrast to the old covenant of the Old Testament. In this new covenant God puts His laws in our minds, that we might know them, and writes them in our hearts, that we might love them. The prophet Ezekiel said of this covenant, "I will put my spirit within you, and cause you to walk in my statutes, and ye shall keep my judgments, and do them" (Ezek. 36:27). The Holy Spirit will cause us to walk in them. This is indeed a vital, spiritual relationship with God. This is holiness. It is not the putting on of something; it is the Spirit enlightening us and empowering and releasing us from within by His presence in our hearts. This is the basis and inspiration for holy living in our world now.

For this—this purity of heart, this strength of life, this singleness of purpose, this covenant life devoted to God, this holiness—God has given us His Holy Spirit.

3. The call to holiness is *a call to wholeness* or wholesomeness. This thought is stressed by Paul in these words: "And the very God of peace sanctify you wholly; and I pray God your whole spirit and soul and body be preserved blameless unto the coming of the Lord Jesus Christ" (1 Thess. 5:23).

He is addressing persons who needed wholeness, persons to whom he had said, "This is the will of God, even your sanctification"; and, "God hath . . . called us . . . unto holiness" (4:3, 7). These were Christian people, as the first three chapters of this letter indicate clearly. But they lacked wholeness. The same is true of many Christians today, and to them God is now speaking through Paul.

One of the most interesting factors about human life is that each of us is not a single self. Rather he is a multiple of selves, a sort of committee of selves within himself. At times there is a clash of these selves with each other. Hence there is not wholeness or unity at the center of life. Each of these selves calls for different attitudes and responses from us.

There is *a home self*—a parental self, a family self. This is the individual in his relation to those people nearest and dearest to him. It is here that he may be seen both at his worst and at his best. There is *a neighborhood self*—the individual in relation to his neighbors. Included in this are his responses to his civic responsibilities and his general attitude toward and conduct in his citizen obligations. There is *a business self*—the individual in relation to people in doing business. This may be as a customer, as a salesperson, as an owner, etc.

There is *a social self*—the individual in his social life. This includes contacts with relatives, with close friends, with casual acquaintances, and general association with people in everyday living. There is *a religious self*—the individual in relation to God, to his church, to church leaders, to other Christians. The total religious bearing of his life as it relates to people in general is involved. There is *the automobile-driving self*—the individual behind the wheel of a car. Does he aim it or drive it? Included here are his attitudes manifested toward other drivers, his reaction to holdups in traffic, his response in situations where courtesy and consideration are called for, etc.

He has *a financial self*—the individual in his total attitude toward money and possessions. This means the getting of it, using it, giving it, sharing it, or hoarding it. It has to do with one's generosity or his spirit of greed, etc. There is *a working or professional self*—the individual in relation to his ways of making a living. This involves his employer, his fellow workers, the kind of work he does, and his professional activities, be he teacher, physician, lawyer, banker, realtor, preacher, etc. There are many other facets to this selfhood which may describe the individual in the various relationships of his life, each of which calls from him different attitudes and responses.

Each of us can say, to some degree at least, "I am these selves." But can we also say, "I am a whole self," with these different facets of my selfhood fitting harmoniously together? Or are there clashes between these different selves, conflicts of loyalties within certain phases of their manifestations? For example, a Sunday school teacher remarked to his pastor, "I am glad none of my class members were present in my home just before we left for church." He was admitting a weakness in his "home self."

A man with several stickers on his car which indicated he might be a Christian was involved in a minor accident. His reaction as a driver was anything but consistent with that profession—a clash within himself.

So it may be with other persons in their many-faceted selfhood. Perhaps they exhibit Christian virtues in some but lack them in others. A secular attitude more than a spiritual attitude may prevail. When one is torn between the conflicts of loyalties to the different selves, it is little wonder that there is so much distress. Someone described it as "a whole civil war going on in my life." There is not wholeness at the center of such a life.

God calls us away from this fragmented way of living to wholeness, to holiness. This wholeness is brought through the working of "the very God of peace." This goes beyond our own disciplinary acts, heroic though they may be. When the Holy Spirit sanctifies wholly, He brings the various facets of the person into a harmonious whole.

How is this wholeness found? It calls for an honest appraisal of ourselves in every phase of our living. It requires, without alibis, a serious facing up to the facts of our selfhood in all of life's relationships—family, neighbors, etc. Here is where the prayer of the Psalmist fits perfectly:

Examine me, O God, and know my thoughts;
test me, and understand my misgivings.
Watch lest I follow any path that grieves thee;
guide me in the ancient ways.
—Ps. 139:23-24, NEB

As God searches our hearts and indicates the points of friction, the low spots, the clashes within, let us accept them and bring them out into the open. We need to acknowledge the truth and recognize our weakness in relation to them. There is no reason to be discouraged under God's examination; just stay with Him until He has shown us ourselves as He sees us. Let us thank Him for His love and rebuke, for His patience and faithfulness, and for His desire to change us. It is His will to sanctify us wholly and thus make us whole persons.

Whatever God shows us, it is our true selves. We may not like what we see, but God is doing it for a reason; that is, to bring us into a wholeness of selfhood. There will be humility and penitence, requesting and accepting God's forgiving grace. We do the one thing needful to find wholeness by completely consecrating ourselves to God, that He may cleanse, strengthen, and unite our many-faceted selfhood into one unity.

Paul expresses his desire for the Thessalonians when he says, "I pray God your whole spirit and soul and body be preserved blameless unto the coming of our Lord Jesus Christ" (1 Thess. 5:23). This suggests that the wholeness the God of peace gives through His sanctifying grace is a real and growing experience in life. It begins as a work of God and continues as we permit Him to work in and through us, keeping or preserving us in wholeness. As responsible Christians, we nurture this relationship with the Spirit by being faithful to the spiritual disciplines in the fellowship of the Spirit. This includes our relationships with other Christians in the Church. Paul wrote:

> *We beg you, brothers, to pay proper respect to those who work among you, those whom the Lord has chosen to guide and instruct you. Treat them with the greatest esteem and love, because of the work they do. Be at peace among yourselves. We urge you brothers: warn the idle, encourage the timid, help the weak, be patient with all. See that no one pays back wrong for wrong, but at all times make it your aim to do good to one another and to all people. Be happy always, pray at all times, be thankful in all circumstances.*

This is what God wants of you, in your life in Christ Jesus. Do not restrain the Holy Spirit; do not despise inspired messages. Put all things to the test: keep what is good, and avoid every kind of evil (1 Thess. 5:12-22, TEV).

We continue in this wholeness by living in this confidence, "Faithful is he that calleth you, who also will do it" (v. 24). That is, the very God of peace who now sanctifies you wholly will keep your whole person—spirit and soul and body—blameless unto the coming of our Lord.

We are living in a society in which life is fragmented. People are "going to pieces," living without purpose or meaning, torn apart and empty, having nothing to live for. Added to this is the uncleanness of our age, which is a symptom of its moral and spiritual sickness. The slavery to alcohol and drugs with the attendant wreckage of human life is part of the scene. People, especially young people, are rebelling against the superficiality and hypocrisy of society, its secular and material ways of living, and its almost total engrossment with things.

Holiness, wholeness, spiritual health through relationship with the Holy Spirit, is the only hope for people in this state of life. It alone brings the necessary unity and healthy attitude into life, which includes a wholesome attitude toward God, toward ourselves, toward other people, toward things and the world in general. It ties life together within the will and love of God, making life satisfying and useful. Its healing reaches into all areas of the person as spirits are made free from tormenting fears and other evil emotions. Healthy minds are filled with the desire to love and serve God and others unselfishly; minds filled with those "things that are good and deserve praise: things that are true, noble, right, pure, lovely, and honorable" (Phil. 4:8, TEV).

This wholeness means oneness with God. The estrangement which once existed is gone; the inner conflict has been resolved. Instead there is a feeling of at-homeness, a realization of "this is where I belong," that "this is what I was made for." It is something like "putting the leaves back on the tree of life."

God calls us to holiness *now* amid all the bad conditions that exist in our world. He is calling us to be His very own people, freed by the presence of the Holy Spirit to be fully devoted to Him. He wants us to be examples of His saving grace, both in the way we live and in the way we respond to people around us as we share His love and blessing with them.

In the life of holiness we have found the only cure for the conditions of evil which plague our society. We must demonstrate its power and make known its truth to the world.

He Gives to Us His Holy Spirit

Living a holy life is possible through our living in relationship to the Holy Spirit. In giving us the Holy Spirit, God brings a new dimension to our lives. Through His active presence with us He enables us to live, to act, and to serve God and others in ways we could not without Him. This means that we are involved with Christ in His work in our world.

If Christ were in our world today in physical presence, He would be just where He was when He was here on earth —right in the midst of its uncleanness. He would be bringing to people His light and truth and healing. He would be sharing His message of hope and salvation. He would be using His power to deliver people now bound by Satan— the alcoholics, the drug addicts, the broken-spirited, the defeated people who are wondering if life is at all worthwhile. It is right there where He wants us to be—you and me who are His present representatives in our world. God's people must go into the uncleanness of our world to bring light and hope and blessing and salvation to people whose lives are dark, empty, and hopeless.

The presence of the Holy Spirit in our lives is God's answer to our feeling of aloneness. He places God's ability over against our inability. He is God's Answer to our weaknesses and inadequacies in moments when we are almost overcome with discouragement. He helps us to overcome our fears, for "God hath not given us the spirit of fear; but of power, and of love, and of a sound mind" (2 Tim. 1:7). In other words, God gives us the Holy Spirit to provide us with everything we need, regardless of our situation, to meet life in confidence and boldness. His presence in and with us makes the difference between our meeting these situations courageously or in frustration.

God is the Giver of the Holy Spirit to us. With this Gift, He offers everything we need for the life of holiness. But *no gift is complete until it is accepted. Receive* is the important word. It is our response to what God offers. *Receive* is God's way for us to have the Holy Spirit come into our lives. Again and again this is emphasized in the New Testament. Let us note some of these statements:

Jesus, just after His resurrection, said to His disciples as He met with them, "Receive the Holy Spirit" (John 20:22, RSV). In answer to the question asked by many on the Day of Pentecost, "Men and brethren, what shall we do?" Peter said: "Repent, and be baptized every one of you in the name of Jesus Christ for the remission of sins, and ye shall receive the gift of the Holy Ghost" (Acts 2:38). The converts from Philip's revival in Samaria through the ministry of Peter and John "received" the Holy Spirit (Acts 8:15, 17). The first statement (v. 15) expresses the purpose of their coming to Samaria; the second

(v. 17) indicates the Samaritans' reception of the Spirit. The Gentile believers at the house of Cornelius "received the Holy Spirit" (Acts 10:47, RSV). Paul asked the believers at Ephesus, "Have ye received the Holy Ghost [Spirit] since ye believed?" (Acts 19:2). Paul asked the Galatian Christians, "Received ye the Spirit by the works of the law or by the hearing of faith?" (Gal. 3:2). This last statement tells us that we receive the Spirit by the hearing of faith. There is no other way.

If our hearts and minds are filled with other things, or with negative thoughts, we cannot receive or experience the Holy Spirit. We receive Him only when in utter trust in God we open our needy lives, our hungry hearts to Him and accept the Gift He is offering us.

In a home in which I was visiting I noticed a gift-wrapped package. I said, "It looks like someone is going to receive a gift." The lady of the home replied, "Oh, that's a gift for C——, but I forget to take it to her." It was only a potential gift, an intended gift, until it was received by the person for whom it was intended. The gift was complete when this person received it. In the realm of the spiritual there are Christians who live only in the area of a potential gift. They appreciate the thoughtfulness of the Giver, but they do not receive God's gift for them which is the fullness of the Holy Spirit.

It comes down to this: Is God trustworthy enough for me fully to trust Him to do what He promised to do for me? Will He give me the gift He has for me? If so, I will now receive the Holy Spirit in His fullness into my life. As I receive His gift, I know He sanctifies me wholly. Through trusting Him as a Person, I, as a person, experience Him and His working in my life.

This giving of the Holy Spirit is stated in the present tense, as late translations indicate. Who gives us the Holy Spirit? God, who calls us to holiness. Dr. William Neal says of this: "To reject God's call is not to offend against Him who at one time bestowed the gift of His Spirit, but it is to sin against the living presence within you of the Holy Spirit which God is giving you every day."[1]

Day by day God is giving us the Holy Spirit. Along with Him, He gives His power, His strength, the fruit of the Spirit. He continually sheds the love of God abroad in our hearts. As we respond to Him, all that Jesus said the Holy Spirit would be and do when He came is ours. He is the Comforter, the Strengthener, the "One alongside" to help us. He will teach and guide us, and make Jesus known to us as a reality in our lives. All that Jesus has provided through His life, His death, His resurrection, and His present intercession for us is made available. He will give us His power to live and serve in our world. He will be our ready Aid when we are pressed hard by the enemy. This continued giving of the Spirit to us is our assurance of our being kept clean in this dirty world, and of our being able to fulfill in life the call of God to holiness.

The measure of our receptivity determines just how much of the Spirit we receive and what He does for us in our living day by day. Is He trustworthy enough for you to trust Him daily, yea, moment by moment? For if we "trust and obey," we will not become the victims of our age.

Chapter SIX

We Belong to God

We belong to God. We belong to Him because He has given us the privilege of giving ourselves to Him as a love-gift. It is most important for us to keep this fact in mind always, for this will help us to overcome in otherwise overwhelming experiences.

There is another fact which we must put alongside this, namely, that we belong to our age, too. True, we are not *of* the world, as Jesus said, but this does not alter the fact that we are *in* or belong to our world. We must live in it as people who belong to God. And indeed many of us find it an exciting age. Despite its evils, this is an exciting age in which to live. An age of great opportunity is ours in which to invest our lives for Christ.

Our world is a shrunken world. Within a matter of hours we can reach most areas of the world. It no longer startles us to hear someone say, "I left Tokyo last night," or, "I have an appointment in London in the morning." Our world in reality is a world neighborhood. The old horizons are gone. We have even watched men of our earth land on and explore the moon. Through means of television and radio we have extended our sight and hearing until within minutes we know about events which are happening in almost any area of the world. We are moved, many times involuntarily, by the news accounts shown and reported. We are moved by the human suffering and death of people in far-off countries, by the violence and bloodshed, and by the horrors of war which are occurring in our world. We are shocked and made anxious by the violence at home, the racial struggles, the breakdown of moral standards, the wide use of drugs and alcohol, and the diseases related to the immorality of this generation. We are disturbed by the turning away from God and religion by so many. We are made to realize that the people caught up in these conditions have found no sure foundation for wholesome living; their lives are rootless, empty, and without meaning or significance. They have really nothing worthwhile to live for. Well, like it or not, we are a part of this world and we cannot evade its influences.

The evils of the age invade the homes and lives of even God's choicest people. Deep suffering and anguish have been brought to them either directly or through relatives and close friends. Divorce has become more prevalent. Alcoholism is claiming more and more victims. Drug addiction is a growing problem, with all its related evils and consequences. Young people join hippy communes, or are involved in illicit sex. Distraught parents ask: "Where did we fail?"

These experiences are happening to the best and most devout Christians. Again and again we are made to realize that we do belong to our age and as a result we suffer from its evils invading our lives and homes. There is no guarantee against this invasion; it could happen to any of us.

Does God Have a Word for Us?

Paul, writing to the Christians in Rome, said:

With eyes wide open to the mercies of God, I beg you, my brothers, as an act of intelligent worship, to give him your bodies as a living sacrifice, consecrated to him and acceptable by him. Don't let the world around you squeeze you into its own mold, but let God remold your minds from within, so that you may prove in practice that the plan of God for you is good, meets all his demands and moves toward the goal of true maturity (Rom. 12:1-2, Phillips).

Paul gives three ways to face the world successfully: (1) Give God your bodies "a living sacrifice, consecrated to him and acceptable by him"; (2) "Don't let the world around you squeeze you into its own mold"; (3) "Let God remold your minds from within."

How are we going to live as we should in this age? Through our truly belonging to God; by having some things so definitely settled deep down in our hearts that, whatever life may bring to us, it will not disturb this essential fact, this true knowledge, that we do belong to God.

The words "Don't let the world around you squeeze you into its own mold" are a challenge to responsible Christians. We realize always that the world's squeeze is on. Our security is found not only in combatting it but also by letting the Holy Spirit fortify us and remold our minds from within.

The Act of Consecration

The Scriptures exhort us to consecrate ourselves to God. "I beseech you therefore, brethren, by the mercies of God, that ye present your bodies a living sacrifice, holy, acceptable unto God, which is your reasonable service" (Rom. 12:1). *The Twentieth Century New Testament* gives this illuminating translation of Rom. 6:13: "Once for all offer yourselves to God (as those who, though once dead, now have Life), and devote every part of your bodies to the cause of righteousness."

Consecration is "an act of intelligent worship" inspired "by the mercies of God." It is a once-for-all act made by one whom Christ has made "alive from the dead," in which the Christian presents himself as an offering to God. It is an intense personal encounter with God. In this special moment of worship, through the help of the Holy Spirit, he makes a deliberate and thoughtful act of offering himself once for all to Him. Henceforth he belongs to God.

The appeal for the Christian to present himself to God is based on *"the mercies of God."* This word is saying that he consecrates because of what God in His mercy has provided for him in Christ Jesus, because He has made him a new person whose life is completely changed, and because he owes all these gracious blessings to Christ, the Saviour. In plain fact, he consecrates his all to God because he loves Him. The purpose of the consecration is that he may love and know Him better. The only compulsion placed upon the Christian is his love for Christ.

The offering he makes is to be *"holy, [and] acceptable to God."* God can use everything good about us and everything that He can make good. We never know how God can use His "living sacrifice[s]" until we commit ourselves to Him and work with Him in fulfilling His will and purpose for us as we live in our world.

Too frequently we leave the false impression that if we "meet the conditions" of entire sanctification we are entering into a sort of transaction with God, that He in return will fill us with the Holy Spirit or sanctify us wholly. It is somewhat like a business transaction: If you will pay me $5.00, I will give you this product. It is no such transaction. This is definitely a personal relationship where love is involved. It is a Christian saying to God: "I am doing this act because I want to express my deep love for You and I can do that in no other way than to consecrate my total self to You." In a sense it is the meeting of conditions which opens our lives to God so that we may be filled with the Holy Spirit. But it is more than our receiving something from God; it is our making a real love-gift of ourselves to Him in a lifetime covenant that He may use us in any way that He desires. As we make this consecration He accepts us, fills us with the Holy Spirit, and sanctifies us wholly.

The appeal is made to *"present your bodies . . . unto God."* Why our bodies? Why not the spirit? Many people think that the body is so sinful and depraved that it has no place as a gift for God. This is not the Christian concept of the body, for we are called upon to glorify God in our bodies and in our spirits which are God's (1 Cor. 6:20). *The body is the total self in its earthly relationships.* We could not adapt ourselves to physical living, to the environment in which we live, without a body. But when we make these adjustments to earthly living through the body we are doing it as total persons. Hence the body, the person living in this world, is to be consecrated to God to be a living sacrifice for Him.

A well-known chorus expresses this act of consecration well:

>*Here I give my all to Thee:*
>*Friends and time, and earthly store;*
>*Soul and body Thine to be—*
>*Wholly Thine forevermore.*
>—WM. MCDONALD

Certainly this expresses the desire and feeling of every true

Christian as in the act of consecration he gives himself to God.

There are two phases to this act of consecration:

1. *It is a decisive and permanent act.* "Once for all offer yourselves to God as those who, though once dead, now have Life" (Rom. 6:13, TCNT). That is, by the help of the Spirit present yourself fully to God in a lifetime dedication. It is something that is settled and final, something which brings a definite direction or set to one's life. Without question one can say, "From now on I belong to God."

This "set" to life settles many things. There is now a definite direction to life. John states this "set" when he says that, if the set of our lives is to walk in the light (to walk with God), certain factors follow. (1) We have fellowship with God and with His people, and (2) the blood of Jesus Christ, His Son, keeps us clean (1 John 1:7).

John goes on to say that this definite set to life, this walking in the light, determines what we do if we are overtaken by sin (2:1-2). Immediately our response is to deplore and repent of the sin. We then humbly, and with confidence solely in Christ, accept complete restoration and continue to walk with Him or to follow the set of our lives. Suppose we set out walking to a desired destination, but somehow along the way we are tripped and fall. What we do about it depends entirely upon our determination to reach our destination. If it doesn't matter much, we turn around and go back. If we are determined to reach the destination, we get up, make any adjustments necessary, and continue on to our goal. When our hearts are set on following Christ, we keep on going no matter how many times we may fall, always humbly asking God's forgiveness and help.

No one *needs* to fall, but anyone *may* fall, even when he is determined to walk with God through life. Someone has said that in such an experience God is there saying to the fallen one just what a loving earthly parent would: "Come on now; get up. If we work together we can make it." The sin has not broken our determination to walk with God, and Christ's intercession for us and His forgiveness have enabled us to continue our walk with Him.

2. *Our consecration to God is a continuing process.* "Devote every part of your bodies to the cause of righteousness." With such diligence we will not be overtaken and defeated by the wickedness and darkness of our age; we will not throw up our hands and think there is nothing we can do. As God remolds our minds from within, we will see situations from His point of view. So motivated, we will live sacrificially for Him who sacrificed so much for us.

We need to become complete persons. When God created man, He said that man was made in the image and likeness of God (Gen. 1:26-27). That image was marred in the fall of man but not destroyed. So if we ever become complete persons we must get back in some way to that relationship and fellowship with God which man was made for. Consecration is a movement in that direction of completeness in relationship with God; we are made for that. This is why God has predestined us "to be conformed to the image of his Son."

Psychologists insist, and human experience confirms it, that we are so constituted that we are never at our best until we find and give ourselves without reserve to something outside ourselves. This must be something greater than ourselves, something which inspires and lifts us above ourselves, something to which we can give our utmost loyalty, something which we find worth living and worth dying for. This something the Christian finds in Someone, Jesus Christ, our Saviour. He alone is worthy of our fullest devotion, our utmost loyalty, and the love of all the heart and soul and mind and strength. It is in Him that we find our utmost fulfillment as persons, our deepest joy for living, and our greatest satisfaction in doing loving service for Him in our world.

Love is a basic factor in consecration. Our love for Christ allows no reservation in the offering we give or the sacrifice we will make for Him. We seek primarily, not an experience, but a deeper personal relationship with Christ through the Holy Spirit. By giving ourselves to Him in the most complete love-gift we can make, we are saying to God, "I love and trust You so fully and have such confidence in You, Your love, and Your wisdom, that I am dedicating myself fully to You to do whatever You may want me to do."

Nor is this love only on our side. We know that He loves us and we are certain that He is accepting us as His very own possession. As Jesus said of His disciples, "They are . . . mine; and I am glorified in them" (John 17:9-10), even so are we. How can we ever fathom this love of God! As He accepts us and our offering, He fills us with the Holy Spirit or sanctifies wholly.

We have previously used the analogy of marriage to picture in some manner our relationship to God in this work of the Holy Spirit. Marriage is also a good analogy for consecration. Normally a marriage is entered into after thoughtful deliberation as an act of mutual love between two persons, each for the other. It is also recognized as being something permanent—"until death do us part." Their love each for the other separates them from all other loves and from whatever is detrimental to the success of the marriage and to the increasing of their love for each other. Marriage is both an act of deliberate dedication to each other and a promise of continuing devotion for each other through a lifetime of fulfilling the commitments made in the marriage covenant.

The relatedness of these factors to consecration is readily noted. It is our love for Christ and our desire to be wholly His that is the reason for our deliberately turning away from self-will, selfish ambitions, and the like to become His alone. We seek and do His will alone in our lives through the help of the Holy Spirit. There is indeed a real separation from everything which is detrimental to this relationship with Christ; there is a dying indeed unto sin, that we may be alive unto God (Rom. 6:11). There is a definite break with the world, its appeals, its values, its standards, and its attitudes toward life. Deep within us there is a conviction that we would rather be consecrated to God and have Him as the Lord of our lives than to have anything else in the world.

Two young ladies were discussing their love affairs. One said she had found the one man for her—the one for whom she would gladly forsake all others to share her life with him. The other responded, "Well, that is fine. I have never found anyone yet for whom I would be willing to make such sacrifices." The truly consecrated Christian has found that One in Jesus Christ. For Him he is willing to make any denial or sacrifice, that he may enjoy a deep relationship with Him, and have the assurance that Christ has accepted him as His very own. What a meaningful life that brings!

Consecration is an act acceptable to God. A Christian Jew who would read the statement of Paul on consecration might call to mind the Temple ceremony where an animal offering is presented by the priests on the altar. To be acceptable as an offering, the animal must have no objectionable characteristics. In this act, the Christian is the priest who presents to God his own body or self upon the altar. It, too, must have no objectionable characteristics. It must be acceptable to God. Since we know God is trustworthy, we can no more think of His rejecting our offering of ourselves to Him than He would have rejected the acceptable sacrifices of His people in olden days. The witness of God's acceptance of us and of our offering is His filling or baptizing us with the Holy Spirit.

Sanctified by Faith

We are sanctified, not by consecration, but by faith. Our full consecration opens the doors of our hearts to believe that Christ indeed does now accept us. In that acceptance He sanctifies us through the baptism with the Holy Spirit.

Some people have a problem at this point. Some would argue, "We cannot be filled with the Holy Spirit until our hearts are made pure." Peter solves that problem in his statement concerning the Gentiles, that God purified their hearts by faith in His act of filling them with the Holy Spirit. Like light dispels darkness, the Holy Spirit purifies the heart.

Over the years the word *faith* has gathered around it many misconceptions. Too often it is thought of as a boy defined it, "Faith is believing that something is true when you know it ain't." Some think that faith is like an old-fashioned automobile tire. If you pump long enough, the tire will be filled with air. Just so, with faith; keep pumping, and you will have enough faith afterwhile. Occasionally the complaint is heard, "I took it by faith and nothing happened." What went wrong? To clarify our thinking and perhaps inspire us to a more intelligent approach, let us consider a synonym of *faith*—the word *trust*.

Trust, like faith, is based upon a personal relationship which inspires a conviction in the trustworthiness of a person. Trust is an act of a person in response to one of whose trustworthiness he is fully convinced. We are sanctified by trust in God. What does that thought do for us? It focuses our attention, not upon ourselves, but upon the trustworthiness of God; being convinced that He is trustworthy, we do trust Him. Trust in God means not only to believe that what He says is true, but that it is true *for us now*. We trust a trustworthy God to do now what He has promised to do. And in the end, when we trust God we are having faith in Him.

In a continuing relationship with Him after we are sanctified, we trust God, who has begun a good work in us, to perform it until the day of Jesus Christ (Phil. 1:6). That is, we trust Him to take us through the conditions which exist in our world today, and to do it in a way which glorifies Him. We believe that His power will keep us until the final day—the day of Jesus Christ.

God's Provision for Us

Through our trust in God we can face our world and even the worst that life can bring to us. Those mysteries which baffle us, those soul-shaking experiences, the disappointments, those events which stagger us—all call for a continuing trust in God. Through them He is opening to us His love, His power, His strength, His grace which is sufficient for us.

As we respond in trust and obedience to God and His keeping power, this relationship with Him is doing something for us. He is remolding our minds from within. He is helping us not to let the world squeeze us into its mold. In other words, we are beginning to see and think more and more in the way God sees and thinks; we are looking at our age and at the experiences we have in it from God's point of view.

The evils of our age, even when they come very close to us, don't upset us. Nor do the bitter experiences we have in the world. Why? Because we belong to God, and His Spirit is at work in our lives. That makes a total difference in our outlook on life. We are in the world, but not of it. We can face these difficult experiences in their stark reality but with trust in God. We can count them as experiences for which God's grace is sufficient to help us overcome, and in such a manner as will bring glory to Him. They will enable us to witness to the difference our relationship to Him makes. We meet these experiences as people who belong to God, God's Spirit-filled people, and we will endeavor by His help to respond to them in ways which will be helpful and redemptive to other persons.

> God himself has said, "I will never let go my grip of you; I will never abandon you." If that be so, we can meet life fearlessly, for we can say: "The Lord is my helper. I shall not be afraid. What can man [or this age] do to me?" (Heb. 13:5-6, Barclay).

What does all of this mean to us? It means that a sanctified or Spirit-filled person, however imperfect he may be in his manifestation of the Christian graces, is a believer. He believes:

1. Although he is a part of his age, he belongs to Christ and he is living in the world in a vital relationship with Him.

2. Christ has accepted him as His very own possession, and that He will never forsake him even when the evils of this age come upon him like a flood.

3. The Spirit of Christ, the Holy Spirit, dwells within him to remold his mind from within and to give him support and assurance in the midst of the worst that life may bring to him. He will not be the victim of his age.

In short: Even though he is a member of this age, he belongs to Christ and with the presence of the Holy Spirit within him he is assured of God's love, His wisdom, His power, and His guidance. He can meet life's difficult experiences in such a way as will honor God.

Chapter
SEVEN

The Day of Pentecost

Pentecost was one of three major annual feasts of the Jews. It was thought to be the commemoration of God's giving the law to Moses on Mount Sinai—a feast to which pilgrims from all over the world came to Jerusalem to celebrate.

The particular Day of Pentecost recorded in the Acts of the Apostles was of most unusual significance, for something happened on that day which changed the world and which brought to full life the Church or body of Christ. This Church under the power and anointing of the Holy Spirit would become the bearer of the good news of salvation through Jesus Christ, the Saviour of the world. What occurred that day has changed everything it has touched —people, cultures, civilizations, nations, the whole world. The power released on this day in the coming of the Holy Spirit upon His people would indeed turn "the world upside down" (Acts 17:6).

Jesus had been preparing His followers for this occasion. He had told them that it was essential for Him to leave them, for through His leaving them He would be able to send the Comforter, the Holy Spirit, to them. He stressed what the Spirit would do in and through them when He came (John 14:16, 26; 15:26; 16:7-15). He related this coming of the Holy Spirit to "the promise of the Father," the fulfillment of which the people of God for centuries had looked for with expectation. The prophet Joel had been the most specific spokesman about the Spirit's coming:

And it shall come to pass in the last days, saith God, I will pour out of my Spirit upon all flesh: and your sons and your daughters shall prophesy, and your young men shall see visions, and your old men shall dream dreams: and on my servants and on my handmaidens I will pour out in those days of my Spirit; and they shall prophesy (Acts 2:17-18).

The words of Jesus relative to this promise were: "Behold, I send the promise of my Father upon you." He told them to wait in Jerusalem for the fulfillment of that promise. Related to this fulfillment, they would be "endued with power from on high," and would be "baptized with the Holy Ghost." To increase their faith and expectation, He said this important event would take place in a few days (Luke 24:49; Acts 1:4-5).

The Day of Fulfillment

The account of what took place in the Upper Room is given in Acts 2 as follows:

And when the day of Pentecost was fully come, they were all with one accord in one place. And suddenly there came a sound from heaven as of a rushing mighty wind, and it filled all the house where they were sitting. And there appeared unto them cloven tongues like as of fire, and it sat upon each of them. And they were all filled with the Holy Ghost, and began to speak with other tongues, as the Spirit gave them utterance (vv. 1-4).

People from far-flung areas of the world heard these Spirit-filled people speak in their own tongues in which they were born. Some asked questions, while others passed off the event with, "These men are full of new wine." Peter, leader of the group, replied: "These are not drunken, as ye suppose." This, he said, was the fulfillment of the words of the prophet Joel. The promise of the Father has come upon His people; "the last days" have come; God has poured out His Spirit upon all flesh. What occurred here was God giving His people what they needed to become His effective messengers for the last days.

Peter further said that what they were seeing was the work of Jesus, the resurrected, glorified Christ: "This Jesus [whom you have crucified] God raised up. . . . Being therefore exalted at the right hand of God, and having received from the Father the promise of the Holy Spirit, he has poured out this which you see and hear" (Acts 2:32-33, RSV).

Jesus, who was crucified and now raised from the dead, was received and exalted to the right hand of God. Now in fulfillment of His promise to His people assembled in Jerusalem, the Holy Spirit was being poured out upon them. This great and wonderful event which they were seeing and hearing was taking place because something great and wonderful was then taking place in heaven. Jesus had been glorified. He was at the right hand of God and was now sharing His triumph and victory in the eternal world with His people by filling them with the Holy

Spirit. God's people on earth were now sharing with Him the victory that was being celebrated in heaven.

By the coming of the Holy Spirit these 120 people were released. They became new persons. A new dimension was given to their lives. The Holy Spirit gave them His power, His wisdom, His help. They began to manifest His presence in their lives in ways they could not have done before. They were indeed released and fulfilled persons.

This meant the fulfillment of the mission of Jesus, a mission which began when He was born in the stable in Bethlehem. That mission continued throughout all His life and ministry and reached its climax in His death and resurrection. His mission now completed, He is exalted to the right hand of God. His life of humiliation as a man is now changed; He is glorified. God has made this Jesus who was crucified both Lord and Christ (v. 36).

It was also the fulfillment of Jesus' promise of the many gracious benefits the Holy Spirit would bring to His people. The Comforter has come to be their Teacher, their Guide, the Revealer of Jesus, and the Dispenser of salvation and redemption. Also there would be the benefits of Jesus' present intercession at the right hand of God. Particularly would the Holy Spirit give them power to witness for Christ (Acts 1:8), and through them He would convict the world of sin (John 16:8).

Who Were Filled with the Spirit?

Those who received the gift of the Holy Spirit at Pentecost were the people of God who were enjoying a definite spiritual relationship with the Lord Jesus Christ. There are many evidences to this fact.

In the prayer of Jesus for His people (John 17) He indicated the relation of these people to himself by saying:

"They are . . . mine; and I am glorified in them" (vv. 9-10). Seven times in His prayer He said they had been given Him by the Father. He said He had kept them, that they were not lost (v. 12), and that they were not of the world (v. 14). He had shared His mission with them: "As thou hast sent me into the world, even so have I also sent them into the world" (v. 18). He had given them the Great Commission, "Go ye into all the world, and preach the gospel to every creature" (Mark 16:15). Earlier in His ministry He had said, "I am the vine, ye are the branches" (John 15:5). They were clean through the word He had spoken to them (v. 3), and He assured them that their names were written in heaven (Luke 10:20). Indeed they were God's people.

The disciples themselves held together even through His passion, and He met with them on the night of His resurrection (John 20:19-22). At that meeting Jesus "breathed on them, and said to them, 'Receive the Holy Spirit'" (v. 22, RSV). This seems to be an "earnest of the Spirit" (2 Cor. 5:5) which they received in fullness on the Day of Pentecost. It was also a certification of their sonship following their checkered experiences during His passion. Jesus met with them frequently after His resurrection and instructed them in things concerning the kingdom of God (Acts 1:5). They obeyed Him and waited in Jerusalem for the promise of the Father (v. 4). Evidently, since there were 120 brethren (Acts 1:15, RSV) who received the fullness of the Spirit, they all in some measure must have shared in these spiritual blessings in their relationship with Jesus.

Since the pattern of Pentecost begins with this fact that believers were filled with the Holy Spirit on the Day of Pentecost, we may assert that the fullness of the Spirit is now an experience for Christian believers only. This is why we stress that the baptism with the Holy Spirit or entire sanctification is a *further* work of the Holy Spirit after His work in regeneration.

Let us look at these disciples from the angle of

THEIR NEED TO BE SPIRIT-FILLED

Some of the actions and attitudes of the disciples as related in the Gospels indicate that, although they were spiritually related to Jesus, there were conditions in their lives which were not pleasing to Him. Often Jesus chided them for their unbelief or little faith. Sometimes it was a rebuke for their failure to have more faith (Matt. 17:17, 20). There was a self-seeking spirit among them as they argued about who of them would be the leaders in the kingdom. Some of this took place even in the Upper Room on the night Jesus instituted the Lord's Supper, just before He went to the Garden of Gethsemane (Luke 22:24-27; Matt. 22:20-24). What an inappropriate time for such a discussion! Even the mother of Zebedee's sons, James and John, came to Jesus requesting that her sons be given favorable positions in His kingdom (Mark 10:35-45).

Their weaknesses became apparent under the pressures of the trial and crucifixion of Jesus. (This stands out in bold contrast to the boldness and courage they exhibited after being filled with the Spirit.) They were dull of spiritual apprehension and slow to understand the teachings of Jesus regarding His death and resurrection. Peter, even after being warned by Jesus, and after he pledged his undying devotion to Him, denied his Lord. But let it be said of him that, even at the time of his denial, Peter was perhaps physically closer to Jesus than any other disciple. At least he was close enough that Jesus could see him, and that look of Jesus brought Peter to deep repentance (Luke 22:61-62).

On the night of His resurrection Jesus met with the

disciples, as we have noted (John 20:19-22), where they were behind closed doors "for fear of the Jews" (v. 19). They knew He had been resurrected, for some of them had seen and talked with Him that day, yet they were hiding from the Jews. Again this is in strong contrast to their fearlessness and courage after Pentecost even when they stood before the very Sanhedrin which had brought about the death of Jesus (Acts 4:13-20).

Certainly if Jesus had to depend upon these people at that time to carry to the world the message of salvation there would not have been much hope of success. But Jesus knew their weaknesses better than anyone else. He knew also that with the coming of the fullness of the Holy Spirit upon them they would be changed men with power to be His witnesses in Jerusalem and to the ends of the earth.

Their Preparation for Pentecost

These followers of Jesus, after they had seen Him ascend into heaven, returned to the Upper Room in Jerusalem, which was the meeting place of the disciples. Luke records that "these all continued with one accord in prayer and supplication, with the women, and Mary the mother of Jesus, and with his brethren" (Acts 1:14). This indicates that they prepared themselves for Pentecost through extended prayer. Note also the unity of spirit—"one accord."

There were some potential blocks in the way which had to be removed. One was the traditional prejudice that Jewish men had toward women. Theirs was a position of servitude. It is said that a Jewish man in those times thanked God each day that he was not born a woman, a Gentile, or a leper. This indicates the status of women in the average Jewish community. But in the Upper Room, Mary, the mother of Jesus, and other women were being accepted as equals with the men as they prepared for the coming of the Holy Spirit. So they were lifted above this potential block of prejudice against women as they waited for Pentecost. Had it not been prophesied that the Holy Spirit would be poured out upon all flesh, and that their sons and their daughters would prophesy? Handmaidens, too, were specifically mentioned. Prejudice is often a block which keeps a person or a church from enjoying the fullness of the Spirit at work in their lives and activities.

There was a potential block in their relation to "the brothers of Jesus" who were in the group. There were four of these brothers, James, Joses, Juda, and Simon (Mark 6:3), but they had not believed on Jesus (John 7:5) before His resurrection. So they were latecomers into the group of believers. The others could have questioned in their minds, Where were you in those years when we followed Jesus with all the opposition and difficulties it brought to us? Why should we now accept you latecomers? But they did not. In their preparation for Pentecost they overcame all suspicion and accepted these brothers of Jesus as their equals in following Christ.

Another potential block was the acceptance of Peter. Some could have asked, "Why should we admit a man into our inner circle who denied the Lord in the presence of unbelievers?" Perhaps there was a personal feeling of guilt for having run away altogether, but there was no rejection of Peter. Their attitude was, If God has forgiven you, if He has restored you, we will give you full acceptance. This reconciliation was so complete that they accepted Peter as their leader.

Thomas could have been a point of conflict. He was not with the group when Jesus appeared to them on the night of His resurrection and he refused to accept their report that the Lord had met with them. Instead, he said,

"'Unless I see in his hands the print of the nails, and place my finger in the mark of the nails, and place my hand in his side, I will not believe'" (John 20:25, RSV). However, one week later Thomas was present when Jesus met with them and was convinced, saying to Jesus, "My Lord and my God." But this group preparing for Pentecost accepted "doubting" Thomas without any reservations.

So in the preparation for Pentecost they swept their prejudices aside and refused to allow any block to exist on their part that would in any manner lessen the glory of the coming of the Holy Spirit in His fullness on the Day of Pentecost.

The Promise Fulfilled

The promise of the baptism with the Holy Spirit was fulfilled on the Day of Pentecost. This meant a great release for them all. "They were all filled with the Holy Spirit and began to talk in other languages, as the Spirit enabled them to speak" (2:4, TEV). They all spoke the message of Christ in languages which the people assembled understood. A mighty miracle indeed!

Look at Peter, this man who in weakness once denied his Lord. He was chief spokesman that day, and so empowered was he that 3,000 believers were added to the Church that very day. It is very evident that Peter, being filled with the Holy Spirit, was released to do what he could never have done before the coming of the Holy Spirit into his life. This was more than something Peter had in himself. Probably no one came to him after that sermon, saying, "Peter, I did not know it was in you." The fact is it was *not* in him; it was the Holy Spirit within him, releasing abilities he already had and adding His power and anointing upon him. The others of the disciple group were also filled with the Spirit and were released and empowered to manifest His presence in ways appropriate to their personalities.

A Corporate Experience

As a result of Pentecost, a spiritual organism was formed, a fellowship in the Spirit—the Church of Jesus Christ was brought to birth. Later Paul in his writings was to call the Church the body of Christ. He likened this body to the physical body—to our hands, feet, ears, eyes, etc.— meaning that each of us has a different place within the total body just as these different organs have different functions within the physical body. By the fullness of the Spirit these different members are able to fit into these different places and perform the functions that are necessary within the Church. Especially in this Pentecostal experience was there a great unity of heart and soul brought to the Church. This is what is said about it:

On that day alone about three thousand souls were added to the number of disciples. They continued steadily learning the teaching of the apostles, and joined in their fellowship, in the breaking of bread, and in prayer. . . . Among the large number who had become believers there was complete agreement of heart and soul. Not one of them claimed any of his possessions as his own but everything was common property to all. The apostles continued to give their witness to the resurrection of the Lord Jesus with great force, and a wonderful spirit of generosity pervaded the whole fellowship (Acts 2:41-42; 4:32-33, Phillips).

These were the people of "the last days." They were people of the Spirit, guided and blessed as a glowing fellowship.

Certainly they are the kind of people needed in these

"last days" in which we live. If we are to make an impression upon our world at all, the Church must have a unity and harmony that comes only through the presence and power of the Spirit within each individual member and within the total group. We need and can have what they experienced in the living presence of the living Lord, a present Person living in us and working through us. Beyond what only a knowledge of theology and the Bible can do (although these have an important place), we need the fullness of the Spirit working in and through our lives, that we may be able to reach the people of our age.

This early Spirit-filled Church was effective in prayer. A crisis developed because of the healing of the lame man at the Beautiful Gate of the Temple through the ministry of Peter and John. These Christian leaders were brought before the Sanhedrin, the very group which had brought about the death of Jesus and still hated everything that was related to Him. This powerful group demanded that Peter and John refrain from preaching and healing in the name of Jesus. Their reply to these demands is inspiring, "'Whether it is right in the sight of God to listen to you rather than God, you must judge; for we cannot but speak of what we have seen and heard'" (Acts 4:19-20, RSV). The Jewish leaders threatened them further and released them.

Peter and John then called the believers together to pray. They began by placing their problem before God in the light of His great creative power and wisdom, and His revelation given through His Word. They concluded by relating their prayer to the present issue:

And now, Lord, behold their threatenings; and grant unto thy servants, that with all boldness they may speak thy word, by stretching forth thine hand to heal; and that signs and wonders may be done in the name of thy holy child Jesus. And when they had prayed, the place was shaken where they were assembled together; and they were all filled with the Holy Ghost, and they spake the word of God with boldness (4:29-31).

This experience was not really another Pentecost. It was God's way of helping the Church meet this critical moment, a new enrichment or outpouring of the Holy Spirit upon these people who were so faithfully standing true to God under this test. The Church today needs such outpourings of the Spirit upon it to make it effective as a witness for Christ in our world. The same is true of its individual members. It was the result of the Church giving itself to earnest prayer.

Later Herod, the ruler, having killed James, the son of Zebedee, thought he would further please the people by killing Peter; so he placed him in prison, where he was to be kept until the feast time had passed. But God's people earnestly prayed for Peter's deliverance and his life was spared in a most remarkable manner (12:5-11).

Blessed is the church which has problems of sufficient import to drive it to its knees before God. For prayer is God's ordained means of dealing with problems and of preparing the Church for effective witnessing for Him.

Another interesting result of Pentecost was that the laymen began to proclaim the gospel. Here is an example:

On that very day [of the stoning of Stephen] a great storm of persecution burst upon the Church in Jerusalem. All Church members except the apostles were scattered over the countryside of Judaea and Samaria. . . . Those who were dispersed by this action went throughout the country, preaching the good news of the message as they went. Philip, for instance, went down to the city of Samaria and preached Christ to the people there (Acts 8:1, 4-5, Phillips).

This was the spontaneous expression from hearts and lives filled with the Holy Spirit. And it would seem to be God's pattern for the Church throughout all ages—preachers and church members alike proclaiming Christ to the people everywhere.

THE PROMISE EXTENDED

On the Day of Pentecost when the people were convicted by the Spirit they asked, "Men and brethren, what shall we do?" Peter told them:

Repent, and be baptized every one of you in the name of Jesus Christ for the remission of sins, and ye shall receive the gift of the Holy Ghost. For the promise is unto you, and to your children, and to all that are afar off, even as many as the Lord our God shall call (Acts 2:38-39).

This means that "the promise of the Father" is extended even to us today. It tells us that the Day of Pentecost as the fulfillment of God's promise to pour out His Spirit upon all flesh is more than a historic, one-day event. It is the day of the Holy Spirit—the day which continues through to "the last days." We live now in the day or age of Pentecost; this is our Day of Pentecost. Everything which the people on that beginning day received which was essential to their relationship to God and to their life and service for Him in our world, we may have now in our Day of Pentecost. The promise includes every Christian until the end of time. What a privilege!

PETER'S EXPERIENCE

This man Peter was one of the first disciples of Jesus.

It appears that his decision to follow the Master fully may have come in a series of contacts with Him. He was introduced to Jesus by his brother Andrew. In this meeting, we are told, "Jesus looked at him, and said, 'So you are Simon the son of John? You shall be called Cephas (which means Peter [a Rock])'" (John 1:41-42, RSV). The next meeting may have been when Jesus, walking along the shore of the Sea of Galilee, saw Simon and Andrew casting a net into the sea. Jesus said to them, "Come ye after me, and I will make you to become fishers of men." And immediately they left their nets and followed Him (Mark 1:16-18).

Another significant experience for Peter took place after Jesus had preached from his boat at the seashore. After preaching He had told Peter to launch out into the deep water and let down the net for a catch. There was a moment of hesitancy, for the men had been fishing all night without catching anything. But, in obedience, Peter and the others with him rowed out and let down their nets. To their amazement they caught so many fish their nets began to break. Impulsively Peter fell down before Jesus, saying, "Depart from me; for I am a sinful man, O Lord." The miracle of the large catch of fish was so overwhelming that it forever settled the matter for Peter and the others as to whether they should follow Jesus or not. They brought their boats to shore, left everything, and followed Him (Luke 5:1-11). There was never a question from then on. Peter was indeed a disciple of Jesus.

Peter became a most important person within the group of disciples; his name always appears first when the names of the disciples are listed. He is generally the spokesman for the group. He it was who voiced the great confession when Jesus asked, "Who do you say that I am?" His reply was, "Thou art the Christ, the Son of the living God." He was the spokesman on the Mount of Transfiguration, when he said, "'Master, it is well that we are here; let us make three booths, one for you and one for Moses and one for Elijah'" (Mark 9:5, RSV).

One time when many of Jesus' other followers had left Him, He questioned the Twelve, "Will you also go away?" Peter affirmed for all their loyalty to Him by saying, "Lord, to whom shall we go? You have the words of eternal life; and we have believed, and have come to know, that you are the Holy One of God" (John 6:66-69, RSV).

Peter with the two sons of Zebedee, James and John, belonged to Jesus' inner circle. They were with Him at the raising of the daughter of Jairus, on the Mount of Transfiguration, and on other occasions. And they were nearest to Him in the Garden of Gethsemane when He engaged in the agony of prayer. Jesus seemed to depend upon them more than upon the others.

Peter had his weaknesses, and Jesus seemed to have a special way of calling them to his attention. On most occasions Jesus spoke of him as Simon Peter or Peter; but when his weaknesses were showing He often spoke to him as "Simon." This term was used in the Upper Room when Jesus was warning him about the wiles of Satan and of his impending denial of his Lord. This was the word used in the Garden of Gethsemane when He found the three sleeping. ("Simon, are you asleep?")

At the post-resurrection appearance on the seashore Jesus' penetrating question to Peter was: "Simon, do you love me more than these?" (RSV). He seemed to be saying, Simon, you are bewildered; you are not able to piece everything together. It all seems so perplexing to you; but where is your heart? "Do you love me more than these?" How tenderly Jesus dealt with him! Simon Peter did pledge his love for Jesus three times, as many times as he had denied Him. He did love Jesus, and he remained His faithful follower until his death.

No doubt Peter's impetuous disposition was a trial to

the patience of Jesus. He seemed so up-and-down. How could Jesus have counted on such a leader when He would leave them? Jesus' love and patience are manifested when on the day of the Resurrection the angel said to the women, "Go, tell his disciples *and* Peter" (Mark 16:7, italics mine).

What a change took place at Pentecost! He was the preacher of the day and spoke with a boldness and clarity which could be attributed only to God speaking through him. Later he showed unusual courage under the most severe trials and pressures from the very people who had brought about the death of Jesus. Always he declared, "We must obey God rather than men" (Acts 4:19; 5:29, RSV). At the very points where once he was weak he now seemed to be the strongest.

In his leadership of the Church he exhibited much poise and strength. His role as judge in the case of Ananias and Sapphira (Acts 5:1-11); his willingness to break the laws of tradition and to obey God in going to the home of a Gentile to preach the gospel (c. 10); and his defense of the Gentile believers before the church council to exempt them from observance of the laws of Moses in order to become Christians (15:6-11); are examples of his unusual wisdom and strength through the Spirit.

Yet he was still human and at times some of the old religious prejudices arose to create problems. All of which tells us that, no matter how well experienced a person may be in the things of the Spirit, on occasion human weaknesses may be manifested.

But there was no more devoted disciple of Jesus, no more fearless evangel and leader in the Early Church, no one who had greater insights into the purposes and will of God for His people than Peter. He is a great historic example of what the fullness of the Spirit in the life of a person can do and what changes He can make when one seriously and responsibly walks with God. It also tells us in loud tones that what God did in the life of Peter through the baptism with the Holy Spirit He can, within the limitations of the person, do in lives of people today when they fully obey and follow Christ.

OTHER PENTECOSTAL EXPERIENCES

The accounts of what God did in the lives of New Testament Christians through their being filled with the Holy Spirit indicate God's pattern of Pentecost, namely, that all Christians need to be led into the deeper commitment or consecration to God which will prepare their hearts for receiving by faith this baptism.

Pentecost marked the beginning of a new age—the age of the Holy Spirit. Other such epochal times were marked by unusual signs, as when God sealed His covenants with Abraham, Moses, and others. The birth of Jesus was accompanied with heavenly signs: His star, the announcement of the angel, and the singing of the heavenly host. So here at the opening of this new age of the Holy Spirit there were symbols accompanying His coming: the sound as of a rushing mighty wind, the cloven tongues like as of fire, and the speaking in other languages plainly understood by the hearers. The signs and symbols are not necessarily repeated, but the promise extended by God through Peter has been fulfilled down through the centuries. As people of God open their minds and hearts to receive the fullness of the Holy Spirit into their lives by faith, He does come in to sanctify wholly.

Other experiences recorded in the Acts of the Apostles concerning the coming of the Holy Spirit follow a definite pattern—the pattern of Pentecost.

The Samaritan Revival (8:5-25)

Out of the persecution of the church at Jerusalem

came a scattering of the Christians throughout the whole area; and wherever they went, they preached Christ. Philip went to the city of Samaria and many people there believed his message and were baptized. When the apostles at Jerusalem heard of this revival, they sent Peter and John to that city to pray for them that they might receive the Holy Spirit. As these apostles laid their hands on them, they did receive the Holy Spirit. You will note that this followed the pattern of the Day of Pentecost—it was a further work of the Holy Spirit.

Saul of Tarsus (9:1-18)

The experience of Saul of Tarsus also followed the pattern of Pentecost. There is no question about Saul's conversion from a persecutor of Christ and Christians into a follower of Jesus in his experience on the Damascus road. So humbled was he there on the road that he asked, "Lord, what wilt thou have me to do?"

Later God directed Ananias to go to see Saul. He did, "and laying his hands on him, he said, 'Brother Saul, the Lord Jesus who appeared to you on the road by which you came, has sent me that you may regain your sight and be filled with the Holy Spirit'" (RSV). Again this followed the pattern of Pentecost—a further work of the Spirit.

The Gentile Pentecost (c. 10, RSV)

The account of the Gentiles of Caesarea receiving the Holy Spirit is inspiring. The Roman centurion, named Cornelius, was "a devout man who feared God with all his household, gave alms liberally to the people, and prayed constantly to God." An angel visited him giving him this assurance, "'Your prayers and your alms have ascended as a memorial before God.'" Then he instructed him to send men to Joppa to find Simon Peter, saying: "'He will declare to you a message by which you will be saved, you and all your household'" (11:14). (The word *saved* is inclusive of the full work of Christ in salvation, even to glorification.)

When Peter arrived at the home of Cornelius, he said to them, "'Truly I perceive that God shows no partiality, but in every nation any one who fears him and does what is right is acceptable to him'" (RSV). Acceptable to Him, "not because of their morality, but by the infinite merit of the Cross, and by the fact that they yielded themselves to the light they possessed."[1] Further, Peter said: "'You know the word which he sent to Israel, preaching good news of peace by Jesus Christ (he is Lord of all)'" (RSV). Evidently Cornelius was not a stranger to the peace which came by Jesus Christ. There seems to be little doubt of the actual spiritual relationship of Cornelius to God. He did indeed "yield himself to the light he possessed."

While Peter preached to these Gentiles, "the Holy Spirit fell on all who heard the word." Again this account follows generally the pattern of Pentecost, with sufficient variations to teach us that God works with people on the level of their ability to understand and not according to a rigid pattern. It was the Gentile "Day of Pentecost."

Believers at Ephesus (19:1-7)

This is the account of Paul coming to Ephesus, where he found 12 "disciples." Noticeable was the fact, however, that they knew nothing of the work of the Holy Spirit. When Paul asked them, "Have ye received the Holy Ghost since ye believed?" they replied, "No, we have never even heard that there is a Holy Spirit" (RSV). Upon further inquiry it was found that they had received only the baptism of John the Baptist. After telling them about Jesus, Paul baptized them in the name of the Lord Jesus. No doubt Paul followed this procedure on the same basis on which Jesus appraised John the Baptist and his ministry. John the Baptist belonged to the old age; Jesus belonged to the new. The baptism of these people was pre-Christian; so when Paul told them of Jesus and gave them Christian baptism, they became Christians. Then, "when Paul had laid his hands upon them, the Holy Spirit came on them" (RSV).

This account follows generally the pattern of Pentecost again with enough variations to indicate God's freedom of working within different situations in appropriate ways.

The pattern of Pentecost is: "They were all filled with the Holy Ghost." There were the disciples of Jesus and other believers on the Day of Pentecost (Acts 2:4); the Samaritan converts (8:15-17); a converted persecutor, Saul of Tarsus (9:17-18); Gentile believers (10:44); and pre-Christian believers after receiving Christian baptism and becoming New Testament Christians at Ephesus (19:6). This baptism with the Holy Spirit is an experience for Christians in which they become released and purified persons filled with the Holy Spirit.

God still works on the pattern of Pentecost. We who are now children of God may, like the believers at Pentecost, "experience that new power of holiness, that peace and love and joy within which the ascended Christ had first given at Pentecost, and is still ready to bestow on all believers."[2] Will we as believers now share in this Pentecostal experience—this baptism with the Holy Spirit? Will we allow the Spirit to fill us with himself until we, like those early believers, find fulfillment in our persons and an adequate life in the Spirit where God meets our needs as we respond to Him in trust? Will we now enjoy the wonderful fellowship in the Spirit as with open hearts we give ourselves through the Spirit to each other within the body of Christ, the Church?

Remember! This is our Day of Pentecost. By our attitude we determine what we now experience and enjoy in life and service from the fullness of the Spirit.

Chapter
EIGHT

The Spirit-filled Life

The Spirit-filled person lives a Spirit-filled life, the life of holiness. This is a life which begins and continues in a vital relationship with the Holy Spirit and through Him with the living Christ. When the relationship is maintained, as indeed it must be, we must not only "grow in grace, and in the knowledge of our Lord and Saviour Jesus Christ" (2 Pet. 3:18); we must also hold our confidence steadfast unto the end, as the Scriptures state:

For we share in Christ, if only we hold fast our first confidence firm to the end (Heb. 3:14, RSV).

And you, who once were estranged and hostile in mind, doing evil deeds, he has now reconciled in his body of flesh by his death, in order to present you holy and blameless and irreproachable before him, <u>provided</u> that you continue in the faith, stable and steadfast, not shifting from the hope of the gospel which you heard (Col. 1:21-23, RSV, emphasis mine).

Need we be worried and troubled because of these warnings? Never. These words challenge us to diligence "in obeying the truth through the Spirit" (1 Pet. 1:22), to hold fast our first confidence firm unto the end, and to continue in the faith. They call upon us to live in the assurance "that he who began a good work in you will bring it to completion at the day of Jesus Christ" (Phil. 1:6, RSV). Also it requires of us to observe the disciplines of the spiritual life as they are stated in the Scriptures.

As we live Spirit-filled lives in our world, we live in the confidence that the Spirit dwelling in us will give us His power to enable us to continue steadfast unto the end.

What Has the Spirit Brought to Us?

The Holy Spirit has given us himself. He is not a fragment of God; He is God in the present tense, so that in Him we have given to us all of God. His total resources are ours for serving Him in this world—all awaiting our receiving and using. In His coming to us He has wrought a wonderful experience in us in which we have passed from the state of regenerating grace into the Spirit's further work of baptizing or filling us with himself. He has sanctified us wholly, and brought us into a life of deeper relationship with Him.

With some people the first awareness of this fullness of the Spirit is a sense of cleanness. "I feel so clean on the inside" is an expression frequently heard. It is significant to note that the continuing fact that remained with Peter, even 12 or more years after Pentecost, was not the sound of the mighty rushing wind, not the cloven tongues of fire, not the speaking in other languages, but rather the fact that God had purified their hearts by faith (Acts 15:8-9). It would seem that Peter thought purity of heart was the primary evidence of the baptism with the Holy Spirit.

The Spirit in this experience brings a new dimension to our lives. The inner conflict between the flesh and the Spirit (Gal. 5:17) has been resolved; there is peace at the center of life. There is also a greater interest in the things of the Spirit, in the Scriptures, in prayer or communion with God, in a loving concern for other people, particularly that they may be brought to know Christ as Saviour. There is an awareness of a fellowship in the Spirit, a fellowship of the saints in love which transcends all human barriers and binds believers together in the unity of the Spirit (Eph. 4:3). There is a new sense of release, a deliverance from former conditions which hindered us in our lives and in our service for Christ. In their place has come a boldness, a realization of the presence and power of the Spirit, a spiritual adequacy which enables us to be effective Christians as we live in our world.

There is also a vital, vibrant fullness of the Spirit in our lives. This is in contrast to the idea that we live in a static state of fullness, where one assumes that having been once filled he remains full throughout his life. This is a false assumption. The fullness of the Spirit is a dynamic fullness, something that increases as we keep our hearts and lives open to the Spirit and as we keep the channels of our lives open to the people of our world.

Throughout the western part of the United States there are vast irrigation systems. A network of large and small canals is kept full to the brim with flowing water during the summer months. These channels carry the water to thousands of acres of orchards, vegetable gardens, and grazing lands to make them productive. This pictures a living, flowing fullness, a vital fullness. It is an analogy of what the Holy Spirit's fullness means to the Christian and to the Church. In turn, God channels His life-giving power and love to the world through His Spirit-filled followers.

It Is a Spirit-filled Life

Previously we have noted some scriptures which stress the epochal experience of being filled with the Holy Spirit, such as on the Day of Pentecost. But there are other scriptures which stress the continuing factor of this experience of the Spirit-filled life. Here are a few of these scriptures, all of which are related to people who had previously been filled with the Spirit in personal experience.

Peter, speaking to the Jewish leaders who were questioning him regarding the healing of the lame man at the Beautiful Gate of the Temple, "filled with the Holy Ghost, said unto them . . ." (Acts 4:8). The whole company of believers as they prayed in a time of crisis "were all filled with the Holy Ghost" (Acts 4:31). There were seven deacons chosen by the Early Church to serve tables while the apostles gave themselves to prayer and to the ministry of the Word. One qualification was that they were to be men "full of the Holy Ghost" (Acts 6:3). Stephen, who was one of these men, at the time of his death, "being full of the Holy Ghost, looked up stedfastly into heaven" (Acts 7:55). Barnabas, we are told, "was a good man, and full of the Holy Ghost" (Acts 11:24). Paul, "filled with the Holy Ghost," brought judgment upon Elymas at Paphos (Acts 13:9).

All of these scriptures indicate a state of life in which the fullness of the Holy Spirit was a vital factor. We, like them, cannot rely upon a one-time experience of the filling with the Spirit; there must be a continual participation in His fullness. Just as the irrigation canals constantly receive from the reservoirs the fullness necessary to make the valleys fruitful, so we need the continual flow of the Spirit's power into our lives.

There are a number of action words used in the Scriptures to describe this participation in the Spirit. One such word is *receive*. The Christians of Galatia "received . . . the

Spirit . . . by the hearing of faith" (Gal. 3:2). *Drink* is another word. We are all "made to drink into one Spirit" (1 Cor. 12:13). Still another is *partake*. We are made "partakers" of the Holy Spirit (Heb. 6:4). The word *walk* is used occasionally. This refers to our everyday employment, activities, and movements; our lives at home, at work, or at school; our pleasures and recreations; our social activities; our total earthly living. The word is used in reference to ongoing Christian life, such as in 1 John 1:7: "If we walk in the light . . . the blood of Jesus Christ his Son cleanseth us from all sin." Or as Phillips translates it: "And the blood which his Son shed for us keeps us clean from all sin."

In relation to life in the Spirit, *walk* is most important. Rom. 8:4 reads, "That the righteousness of the law might be fulfilled in us, who walk . . . after the Spirit," or "as we live and move . . . by the Spirit" (Moffatt). Another passage is: "Walk in the Spirit, and ye shall not fulfil the lust of the flesh. . . . If we live in the Spirit, let us also walk in the Spirit" (Gal. 5:16, 25).

What glorious companionship we have with Christ as we live and move in the Spirit, for the Spirit in us is "the Spirit of Christ" (Rom. 8:9)! All of which calls us to live in the awareness that "your body is the temple of the Holy Ghost which is in you, which ye have of God, and ye are not your own. . . . therefore glorify God in your body, and in your spirit, which are God's" (1 Cor. 6:19-20).

Another action word is *mind,* which refers to the direction of one's thinking. Paul says, "Those who live according to the Spirit set their minds on the things of the Spirit" (Rom. 8:5, RSV). To "live according to the Spirit" seems to be synonymous with to "walk in the Spirit" and to be "spiritually minded." The result of setting the mind on the Spirit "is life and peace."

"Life and peace." These are what people are seeking

today. But many of them are seeking them in the wrong places and by wrong means. Actually they come only through being spiritually-minded or by minding the things of the Spirit.

Life means more than existence. Life which comes from being spiritually-minded is that of which Jesus spoke when He said, "I am come that they might have life, and that they might have it more abundantly" (John 10:10). Someone made this free translation: "I am come that you might have vitality, and that you might overflow with it." This life or vitality which comes from the Spirit is expressive of the Spirit of Christ. It is something spontaneous, dynamic, radiant, with a freedom which makes the Spirit-filled life winsome and attractive. It is overflowing with spiritual vitality.

The word *peace* is often used in a wistful manner, for there seems to be little peace in our world. But peace can be found within one's heart. It is the result of Christians setting their minds on the Spirit, or being spiritually-minded. Peace is more than the absence of strife; it is a state of tranquility, of spiritual contentment. Dr. C. H. Dodd says, "Peace here stands for the condition of inward harmony when all elements are organized about a single center, and division and conflict are at an end."[1] Peace has been said to come from the consciousness of having adequate resources. Spirit-filled Christians know that to have the Spirit is to have all, for everything He is and has is offered to us. The limitations are on our part, for our capacity to understand and to receive is restricted. Even our minding the things of the Spirit may fluctuate. But as we set our minds upon Him, the Spirit who dwells within us gives us everything we need to meet anything that comes to us in our everyday living. Indeed, to set the mind on the Spirit *is* life and peace.

A list of Christian graces found in the Spirit-filled

life is given by Paul in Galatians 5: "The fruit of the Spirit is love, joy, peace, patience, kindness, goodness, faithfulness, gentleness, self-control" (vv. 22-23, RSV). These are the normal manifestations of the presence of the Holy Spirit in persons who "set their minds on the Spirit." They cannot be "put on" by human effort; they are alone the fruit of the Spirit dwelling within the Christian.

Life in Relationship with God's People

We have noted how the body of Christ, the Church, is formed: "By one Spirit are we all baptized into one body" (1 Cor. 12:13). Paul likens this spiritual body, the Church, to the physical body and emphasizes the importance of the proper coordination within that body. The same cooperation should exist within the body of Christ: "That there may be no discord in the body, but that the members may have the same care for one another. If one member suffers, all suffer together; if one member is honored, all rejoice together" (1 Cor. 12:25-26, RSV). In another place he calls this body "the fellowship of the Spirit" (Phil. 2:1). The cement which binds this fellowship together is the "love of the Spirit" (Rom. 15:30; Col. 1:8). Mere human love, as good as it may be, is not sufficient to make the fellowship of Christians what God has planned it should be. The only meaningful fellowship we as Christians can have is when we share that fellowship in "the love of the Spirit." This fellowship in the Spirit overcomes all human barriers and differences to make us one in the Lord.

In this life in the Spirit, *He helps us to pray* and to make our prayer life fruitful:

> *The Spirit also helpeth our infirmities: for we know not what we should pray for as we ought: but the Spirit itself maketh intercession for us with groanings which cannot be uttered. And he*

> *that searcheth the hearts knoweth what is the mind of the Spirit, because he maketh intercession for the saints according to the will of God* (Rom. 8:26-27).

The universal testimony of people filled with the Spirit is that prayer takes on new meaning and is much more fruitful in its results as they cooperate with the Spirit in the life of prayer. This is a necessary part of our progress toward the destiny God has set for us, that we "be conformed to the image of his Son" (v. 29).

Another of the great benefits of life in the Spirit is to help us *live in hope.* Paul wrote the Roman Christians who were living in a world even worse than ours: "May the God of hope fill you with joy and peace in your faith, that by the power of the Holy Spirit, your whole life and outlook may be radiant with hope" (Rom. 15:12, Phillips). What a great prayer for today! Is is easy for us to allow the world around us to smother us in its mood of gloom and despair. But we are children of God, therefore children of hope. William Barclay writes:

> Hope is characteristically the Christian virtue and it is something which for the unchristian is impossible (Eph. 1:12). Only the Christian can be optimistic regarding this world. Only the Christian can hope to cope with life. And only the Christian can regard death with serenity and equanimity.... The Christian hope is not simply a trembling, hesitant hope that perhaps the promises of God may be true. It is the confident, expectant hope that they cannot be anything else but true.[2]

We are not victims of futurelessness. We are confident of the future. We live by "the substance of things hoped for, the evidence of things not seen" (Heb. 11:1). We know that the promises of God speak of a reality which with Him already exists. So we accept the present in the light of what is to come. In other words, we "live from the future," as did Abraham and others who were content to dwell in tabernacles as they looked for "a city which had foundations, whose builder and maker is God." Moses pursued his conflict with Pharaoh in the knowledge that the future held deliverance for God's people and the establishment of their nation. So "he endured, as seeing him who is invisible," but not unreal (cf. Heb. 11:9-10, 26-28).

Jesus himself endured the Cross and despised the shame for the joy that was set before Him—the joy of the future, His exaltation to the right hand of God, a world of mankind redeemed, and a universe eventually freed from all evil (cf. Heb. 12:2). Paul endured the light, momentary afflictions in the future hope of "a far more exceeding and eternal weight of glory" (2 Cor. 4:17-18). The secret was that he saw the reality of the future, and this hope sustained him and gave him strength and courage in his afflictions. We "live from the future," for indeed the future reaches back into our present, giving us "patience of hope," hearts that are established, and lives filled with a labor of love and a work of faith until the coming of our Lord (cf. 1 Thess. 1:3; Jas. 5:7-8).

We move on toward maturity in the Spirit. The goal that God has predestined for us is "to be conformed to the image of his Son." This goal can be reached only through our active participation with the Holy Spirit in a relationship of trust and obedience to bring into our lives those qualities of character which move us toward that goal. We ever need in this relationship to "let God remold . . . [our] minds from within, so that . . . [we] may prove in practice that the plan of God for . . . [us] is good, meets all his demands and moves toward the goal of true maturity" (Rom. 12:2, Phillips). The measure of our cooperation with

God in these matters will determine how our moving toward maturity is furthered.

Within the Church, the body of Christ, the Christian finds an environment which helps him move toward maturity. The symbol of the Church as the family of God (Eph. 2:19-22) is especially meaningful. It is within our natural family through its love and care, its fellowship and guidance, that we develop as persons. It is there we learn to adjust in relationship with other members of the family, and find the advantages provided for growth, development, and maturity which will help us meet the demands of life in the world about us. So it is within "the household [or family] of God," the Church. Similar incentives and opportunities are provided for our spiritual maturation. As we give ourselves to its fellowship in the Spirit and as we grasp the opportunities it offers for the use of our talents and the special gifts of the Spirit given us, we develop more and more as responsible Christian persons. In the process we are increasingly conformed to the image of Christ.

The Gifts of the Spirit

God did not expect His Church to make progress within itself or to be His channel of blessing to the world solely by depending upon its own human talents and resources. Valuable as these might be, He knew human limitations and the need of special divine help. So He provided special spiritual gifts for the Church to make it effective in the mission He has for it. Paul speaks of the gifts of leadership:

> *Through the grace of God we have different gifts. If our gift is preaching, let us preach to the limit of our vision. If it is serving others let us concentrate on our service; if it is teaching let us give all we have to our teaching; and if our gift be*

> *the stimulating of the faith of others let us set ourselves to it. Let the man that is called to give, give freely; let the man who wields authority think of his responsibility; let the man who feels sympathy for his fellows act cheerfully* (Rom. 12:6-8, Phillips).

To another church he wrote:

> *And he gave some as apostles, and some as prophets, and some as evangelists, and some as pastors and teachers, for the equipping of the saints for the work of service, to the building up of the body of Christ; until we all attain to the unity of the faith, and of the knowledge of the Son of God, to a mature man, to the measure of the stature which belongs to the fulness of Christ* (Eph. 4:11-13, NASB).

These gifts and the responsibilities accompanying them are not given for the advantage of the receiver; they are given for the benefit of the entire Church—"until we all attain." Let us note that in verse 12 of this last quotation the comma used in the King James Version between the words "saints" and "for" is missing. This stresses more accurately the intent of the message, that the work of these leaders is to prepare the saints to render service. (The comma is omitted in almost all of the recent translations. The original manuscripts do not have punctuation, so this has to be supplied by translators.) So God calls some to be apostles, etc., that through the faithful use of these gifts the entire church may be brought to the place where the members can do "the work of the ministry." "The work of the ministry" belongs to the entire church as the different members fulfill their Christian responsibilities and use the special gifts of the Spirit given to them.

In his letter to the Corinthian church Paul discusses

the gifts of the Spirit more fully (1 Corinthians 12). He says there are a variety of gifts and that each member is given the manifestation of the Spirit for the good of all (v. 7). The Spirit distributes these gifts to each one individually as He wills (v. 11).

To one person is given the gift of wisdom, and to another the gift of knowledge. There is a fine distinction here. One seems to have the gift of insight into the things of God; the other has the ability to apply it to human living. To another is given faith—not ordinary faith, but the faith Jesus said could remove mountains, the ability to see the invisible and to bring it into fact. To another are given gifts of healing. There are those who seem to have a special gift for bringing *physical* healing, but certainly there is need within the Church for other kinds of healing too— healing of mind, healing of spirit, healing of troubled hearts, healing of troubled families, etc. To another is given the power to work miracles. In the days of the Early Church and in some situations today (particularly on mission fields) this would include power to cast out demons. To another is given the distinguishing of spirits—"ability to distinguish true spirits from false" (NEB).

Later in the chapter Paul lists the gifts in their order of importance: first, apostles (those who were related to Jesus in His life); second, prophets (not so much foretellers as proclaimers, "preachers of power" as Phillips puts it); third, teachers; then workers of miracles; then healers; helpers (those who comfort, strengthen, encourage, and uplift those who need these ministries); administrators (those who care for the everyday business of the church); speakers in various kinds of tongues, "ecstatic utterance of various kinds" (NEB). This last-named vocal gift was apparently much coveted by these infantile Corinthians (cf. 14:20), the use of which caused Paul no little concern.

The final gift named was the interpretation of tongues (necessary whenever tongues were spoken).

To guide the Church in the possession and use of these gifts, God spoke through Paul for all the Church, then and now, the message of love in the thirteenth chapter of this book. Without love everything is useless, and if it is not present no gift is effective for expressing God's message to the world.

What about these gifts in the Church today? Are they needed? The Church, as the body of Christ, is in the same world in which Paul lived, and is endeavoring to do the same work. The needs of people are the same and the same Holy Spirit is present in the Church now. Is there any reason why He should not be giving to the body of Christ the gifts which have made the Church effective in its work in other days?

The gifts of the Spirit are needed today to have the Church fulfill its mission to our world. The question is, Will the Church today be open to receive them? Should we reject all of the gifts of the Spirit just because one gift has been abused, misused, overemphasized, and become troublesome?

What would happen in our world today if each Christian would with open heart receive the gift which God wants to give him? If then in love and diligence he would use that gift for the glory of God and to reach the world with the message of Christ and salvation, how far-reaching the effect would be! It would bring a spiritual awakening to our world such as it has never known before.

If the fullness of the Spirit is to stimulate responsible Christians to accept and use effectively the gifts of the Spirit for the benefit of the entire Church, then we should heed Peter's exhortation: "As each one has received a special gift, employ it in serving one another, as good stewards of the manifold grace of God." Or, "Serve one another with the particular gifts God has given each of you, as faithful dispensers of the magnificently varied grace of God" (1 Pet. 4:10, NASB, Phillips).

God has such faith in us that He gives us His gifts in the confidence that we will use them for others and to help His Church to become what He desires it to be in the world. He calls upon us to have faith in ourselves and in His love and wisdom to make full use of the Spirit's gifts. Instead of our being overwhelmed by such a responsibility we must accept our gifts and use them, that we might become the persons God sees in us. He gave us not only our natural talents but these spiritual gifts for a purpose.

Think of what your church could become if each member would accept these gifts and responsibly and enthusiastically use them for the glory of God, the Giver. The Holy Spirit is within us to give us power and courage and understanding to use them to the fullest extent of our ability.

The Resources of the Spirit

Paul, although he was writing from prison, wrote of his experience in these optimistic terms: "Yes, and I shall go on being very happy, for I know that what is happening will be good for my own soul, thanks to your prayers and the resources of the Spirit of Jesus Christ" (Phil. 1:18-19, Phillips).

What have we to count upon as we live under today's pressures and tensions and endeavor to live Spirit-filled lives in this world? We can count on the fact that ours are not lives of individual struggle and effort, for we live in a conscious relationship with the Holy Spirit who is God in the present tense. We can be as sure as Paul was that whatever "is happening will be good for my soul." Further, we are not living on a hand-to-mouth basis in the spiritual life; we are living in "the resources of the Spirit of Jesus Christ" and we can always count on these. These resources mean for us a bountiful supply of everything we need to make us the kind of Christians which will glorify God and to some degree turn the minds of people about us to thoughts of Christ. The resources of the Spirit are available now and in each and every circumstance of life. We can live victoriously in the supply which is available to us, just as we live physically in God's supply of air for the physical life. Let us be grateful receivers of these resources of the Spirit as we live the Spirit-filled life.

Reference Notes

CHAPTER 1:
1. John Grant McKenzie, *Psychology, Psychotherapy and Evangelism* (London: G. Allen and Unwin, Ltd., 1940), pp. 187-88.
2. R. S. Foster, *Christian Purity* (Nashville: Abingdon Press, 1897), p. 126.
3. *Ibid.*, p. 128.

CHAPTER 3:
1. C. H. Dodd, "Romans," *The Moffatt New Testament Commentary* (New York: Doubleday, Doran and Co., n.d.), p. 74.
2. D. Guthrie and J. A. Motyer, eds., *The New Bible Commentary* (Grand Rapids, Mich.: Wm. B. Eerdmans Publishing Co., 1953), p. 948.
3. Adam Clarke, *Commentary on the Holy Bible* (New York: Abingdon Press, n.d.) 6:37.

CHAPTER 4:
1. R. George Smith, *A Theological Word Book of the Bible,* Allan Richardson, ed. (New York: The Macmillan Co., 1951), p. 167.
2. H. Orton Wiley, *Christian Theology* (Kansas City: Beacon Hill Press, 1952) 2:362-63.

CHAPTER 5:
1. William Neal, "Thessalonians," *Moffatt Commentary,* p. 84.

CHAPTER 7:
1. G. Cambell Morgan, *The Acts of the Apostles* (New York: Fleming H. Revell Co., 1924), p. 134.
2. J. R. Dummelow, ed., *A Commentary on the Holy Bible* (New York: The Macmillan Co., 1936), p. 820.

CHAPTER 8:
1. Dodd, "Romans," *Moffatt Commentary,* p. 122.
2. William Barclay, *More New Testament Words* (New York: Harper and Row, 1953), pp. 42-46.